The MAILBOX

The Education Center

Fascinating Facts
SCIENCE
100 Comprehension-Building Activities

W9-BJJ-754

- **Survival and Adaptation**
- **Ecosystems**
- **Weather**
- **Rocks and Minerals**

- **Earth's Surface**
- **Solar System**
- **Matter**
- **Energy and Motion**

Also includes a ready-to-use review game!

Managing Editor: Peggy Hambright

Editorial Team: Becky S. Andrews, Kimberley Bruck, Karen P. Shelton, Diane Badden, Thad H. McLaurin, Debra Liverman, Marsha Erskine, Amy Payne, Karen A. Brudnak, Juli Docimo Blair, Hope Rodgers, Dorothy C. McKinney, Juli Engel, Joanne Mattern, Kim Minafo, Jennifer Otter, Christine Thuman

Production Team: Lori Z. Henry, Pam Crane, Rebecca Saunders, Jennifer Tipton Cappoen, Chris Curry, Sarah Foreman, Theresa Lewis Goode, Greg D. Rieves, Eliseo De Jesus Santos II, Barry Slate, Donna K. Teal, Zane Williard, Tazmen Carlisle, Marsha Heim, Lynette Dickerson, Mark Rainey, William Shawn Pegram, Teresa Uhls

www.themailbox.com

Manufactured in the United States
10 9 8 7 6 5 4 3 2 1

Table of Contents

Survival and Adaptation

Ecosystems

Weather

Rocks and Minerals

Earth's Surface

Solar System

Matter

Energy and Motion

What's Inside

100 Reproducible Activities

Inside this book, you'll find activities that support 50 essential science topics. Each topic is reinforced with two engaging reproducible activities that can be used together or separately.

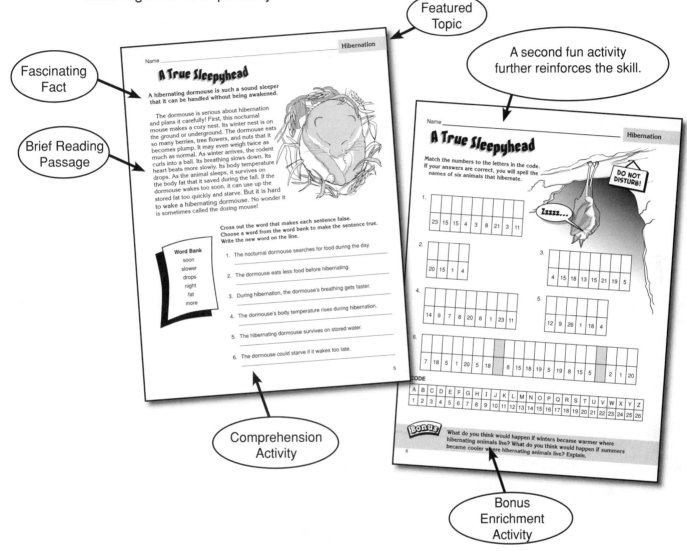

Featured Topic

A second fun activity further reinforces the skill.

Fascinating Fact

Brief Reading Passage

Comprehension Activity

Bonus Enrichment Activity

Ready-to-Use Trivia Game

On pages 105–120, you'll find an exciting trivia game containing 150 cards that review all 50 topics covered in this book. Use the game to review just one topic or use all the cards as a fun year-end review. The game cards also make great flash cards for review.

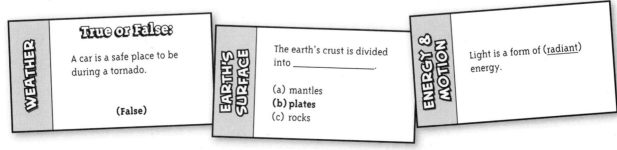

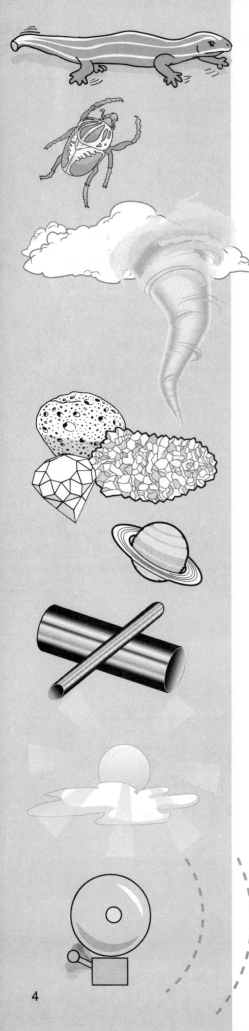

How to Use

Use *Fascinating Facts: Science* as

- morning work
- a center activity
- homework
- enrichment
- remediation
- work for early finishers
- small-group practice
- independent practice

Use *Fascinating Facts: Science* to

- engage students in the learning of science
- integrate reading with science
- provide independent practice of key science concepts
- strengthen comprehension of nonfiction texts
- provide extra practice for struggling readers
- introduce a new science topic
- review content before a test
- provide practice with answering questions in different formats

A True Sleepyhead

A hibernating dormouse is such a sound sleeper that it can be handled without being awakened.

The dormouse is serious about hibernation and plans it carefully! First, this nocturnal mouse makes a cozy nest. Its winter nest is on the ground or underground. The dormouse eats so many berries, tree flowers, and nuts that it becomes plump. It may even weigh twice as much as normal. As winter arrives, the rodent curls into a ball. Its breathing slows down. Its heart beats more slowly. Its body temperature drops. As the animal sleeps, it survives on the body fat that it saved during the fall. If the dormouse wakes too soon, it can use up the stored fat too quickly and starve. But it is hard to wake a hibernating dormouse. No wonder it is sometimes called the dozing mouse!

Cross out the word that makes each sentence false.
Choose a word from the word bank to make the sentence true.
Write the new word on the line.

Word Bank

soon

slower

drops

night

fat

more

1. The nocturnal dormouse searches for food during the day.

   _____

2. The dormouse eats less food before hibernating.

   _____

3. During hibernation, the dormouse's breathing gets faster.

   _____

4. The dormouse's body temperature rises during hibernation.

   _____

5. The hibernating dormouse survives on stored water.

   _____

6. The dormouse could starve if it wakes too late.

   _____

A True Sleepyhead

Match the numbers to the letters in the code.
If your answers are correct, you will spell the
names of six animals that hibernate.

DO NOT DISTURB!

Zzzzz...

1.

23	15	15	4	3	8	21	3	11

2.

20	15	1	4

3.

4	15	18	13	15	21	19	5

4.

14	9	7	8	20	8	1	23	11

5.

12	9	26	1	18	4

6.

7	18	5	1	20	5	18		8	15	18	19	5	19	8	15	5		2	1	20

CODE

A	B	C	D	E	F	G	H	I	J	K	L	M	N	O	P	Q	R	S	T	U	V	W	X	Y	Z
1	2	3	4	5	6	7	8	9	10	11	12	13	14	15	16	17	18	19	20	21	22	23	24	25	26

Bonus   What do you think would happen if winters became warmer where
hibernating animals live? What do you think would happen if summers
became cooler where hibernating animals live? Explain.

A Long Journey

Gray whales travel over 10,000 miles a year!

In the summer, gray whales bask in the northern Pacific Ocean. These giant sea mammals eat tiny sea creatures, such as krill, that thrive there during the summer. A whale feasts on over a ton of krill a day! This helps the whale build up a thick layer of fat, or blubber. The whales need blubber to live on during their long journey southward. They travel more than 5,000 miles to the warm waters of western Mexico. Here, the mother whales give birth to their calves. Baby whales then drink milk from their moms. This builds a layer of blubber on the calves. In the spring, the babies swim back with the group to the same cold northern waters. There the gray whales again feast on the shrimplike krill. This migration happens year after year.

Use the passage to answer the questions.

1. How much krill can one gray whale eat each day? _____

   _____

2. About how many miles do whales travel from the northern Pacific Ocean to the waters near western Mexico? _____

3. Why do gray whales need blubber?_____

   _____

4. Why do you think gray whale calves are not born in the northern Pacific Ocean? _____

   _____

A Long Journey

Match each cause to its effect.

Causes

_____ 1. During migration, gray whales live mostly on the fat that was stored during the summer.

_____ 2. During the winter, whale calves grow a thick layer of blubber.

_____ 3. Whale hunting has declined since the 1930s.

_____ 4. A gray whale eats more than 2,000 pounds of krill a day in the summer.

_____ 5. Gray whales swim near the shore when they migrate.

Effects

A. Whale watching is a popular activity.

B. Gray whales build a thick layer of blubber.

C. The whales eat little, if any, food while they travel.

D. In the spring, the calves are ready for the long trip north.

E. There are more gray whales today than there were in the early 1900s.

Bonus: What is an advantage of the whales migrating in a group?

A Frightening Act

The Australian frilled lizard bluffs its way out of danger.

Big, noisy creatures are scary. The Australian frilled lizard must know this. In tree branches, the three-foot-long lizard might be overlooked. Its skin blends in with the bark on the trees where it likes to live. But when it moves to the ground to eat, it may face danger. Then the frilled lizard unfolds its neck frill. The frill looks like an open umbrella around its head. The brightly colored ruffle of an adult male can be about nine inches across! That is about the size of a small dinner plate. The lizard also hisses and shows its teeth and the yellow lining of its mouth. It also tries thumping its long tail on the ground to bring about fear. This frightful display scares many foes away. If this bluff does not work, the lizard runs to a nearby tree branch for safety.

Circle the correct word to complete the sentence.

1. The adult male frilled lizard has a (large, small) frill.

2. When threatened, the lizard expands its brightly colored (frill, umbrella). It also opens its (frill, mouth).

3. The lizard may even (curl, thump) its long tail.

4. The frill makes the lizard seem (bigger, unnoticed).

5. If a foe is not afraid of the frilled lizard's actions, the lizard (flies, runs) away.

Name _____

10

A Frightening Act

Read the passage on page 9.
Decide whether each statement is true or false.
Then color the correct foot print.

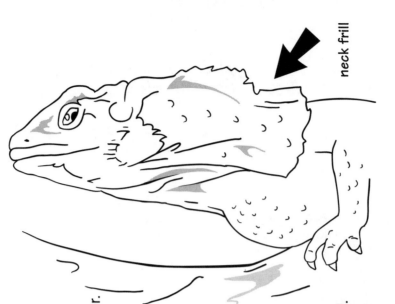

neck frill

TRUE   **FALSE**

1. The frilled lizard's yellow mouth can be seen when the lizard is in danger.

2. The unfolded neck frill of the female is large.

3. If the scare tactics of this lizard fail, it will fight its predator.

4. The frilled lizard expands its neck frill when in danger.

5. A hiding place for this lizard is among the fallen leaves.

6. A frilled lizard's tail is too large to move quickly.

7. The three-inch-long frilled lizard is too small to be seen unless provoked.

8. The teeth of a frilled lizard can be seen when it is in danger.

BONUS

Explain what might happen if this lizard lost its skill to frighten off a predator.

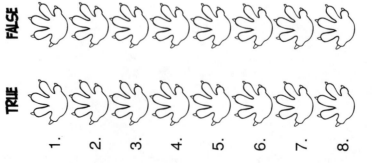

Copycats

The viceroy butterfly tricks birds into thinking it is a not-so-tasty treat!

viceroy butterfly

Have you ever been told you look like someone else? Some animals look like, or mimic, others to fool predators. Viceroy and monarch butterflies look a lot alike. At least, birds think so. The viceroy is about the same size, shape, and color as the monarch. When a bird bites into a monarch butterfly, it quickly learns to stay away. It is believed that the monarch tastes bad to birds. The shared likeness with the monarch allows the viceroy the freedom to eat without as much worry of being eaten. That has to be a big relief to the viceroy, don't you think?

Circle the correct answer.

1. Which butterfly is believed to taste bad to birds?
   a. monarch
   b. viceroy
   c. both

2. How does mimicry help the viceroy butterfly?
   a. People admire the colors of the butterfly.
   b. It helps protect the butterfly from foes.
   c. It helps it blend with the flowers nearby.

monarch butterfly

3. When a bird bites into a monarch butterfly, the bird _____.
   a. wants to take another bite
   b. learns that this butterfly tastes bad
   c. sings a special song

4. When an animal looks like another animal in color, shape, or size, it is called _____.
   a. mimicry
   b. dress-up time
   c. hibernation

Name _____

Copycats

Word Box

LEAF INSECT
DRONGO BIRD
ANGLERFISH
KING SNAKE
MONARCH BUTTERFLY
FLY ORCHID
HOVERFLY
NEMORIA ARIZONARIA
   CATERPILLAR

Fill in the blank with the correct word from the word box.

1. This animal looks like the poisonous coral snake
   ☐☐☐☐ ☐☐☐☐○

2. This insect is hard to see when it is on green leaves.
   ☐☐☐☐ ☐☐○☐☐

3. The fuzzy spring blooms on an oak tree help this fuzzy insect hide from birds in the spring.
   ☐☐☐☐☐☐☐ ☐☐☐☐☐☐☐☐☐
   ☐☐○☐☐☐☐☐☐

4. The viceroy butterfly looks like this insect. ☐☐☐☐☐☐○
   ☐☐☐☐☐☐☐☐☐

5. The black flycatcher looks like this bird that tastes bad to predators.
   ☐☐☐☐☐☐ ☐○☐☐

6. This flower attracts the male tachinid fly. It has the same colors and shape as the female tachinid fly. ☐☐☐ ☐☐☐☐○☐☐

7. To hide from predators, this fish looks like the rocks on the ocean floor.
   ☐☐☐☐☐☐☐☐☐○☐

8. Predators avoid this insect because it looks like a stinging yellow jacket. ☐☐☐☐☐☐☐○

How do termites imitate a snake and scare away predators?

To find out, write the circled letters above on the matching lines below.

___ ___ ___ ___   ___ ___ ___ ___!
 3   4   1   8   6   5   2   7

Bonus
Choose any animal. Describe how mimicry might help it survive.

DISGUISED!

The stick insect looks, moves, and falls to the ground much like a twig.

Do you ever wonder what you will look like when you grow up? If you were a stick insect, you would look like a twig! This insect is sometimes called a walking stick. Its long, slender body matches the colors of the plants it eats. To spot one, you need to live in a tropical or temperate climate. You should also have a flashlight because the walking stick feeds only at night. It tries to stay still during the day when predators are hunting for food. As it eats grasses and the leaves of trees and bushes, it moves slowly to avoid being seen. If threatened, it sways gently like a stick being blown by the wind. It may even pretend to be a broken twig and fall to the ground. If that does not work, it flies away!

Unscramble the letters in parentheses to spell a word. Then write the word in the blank.

1. The walking stick lives where the climate is _____ or temperate. (caportil)

2. This insect is nocturnal, or active at _____. (gnith)

3. It uses camouflage to avoid _____. (trpdasero)

4. Sometimes, it sways gently to mimic a twig being blown by a _____. (zeeber)

5. The walking stick may drop to the ground like a broken _____. (giwt)

DISGUISED!

Read the clues about some animals that disguise themselves.
Unscramble the letters in parentheses.
Then circle the answers in the puzzle below.

1. This reptile looks like a vine. Its tongue looks like an insect. (nive aeksn) _____

2. This creature never spins a web. It hides in a flower to capture its dinner. (brca rsepdi) _____

3. The flesh of a spotted scorpion fish makes it look like an algae-covered rock on the ocean floor. It uses these to protect itself. (nipses) _____

4. This animal looks like a floating log. (cocordlie) _____

5. This sea fish uses its body to look like a cave. Then it eats the small fish that are trapped inside. (yra) _____

6. The blenny fish swims and looks like a harmless cleaner fish. It mimics the cleaner fish to get close enough to do this to its prey. (tieb) _____

g	n	l	e	t	i	b	s	s	c	t	w	a	e
e	l	o	c	o	r	s	o	e	r	n	l	b	c
q	z	l	s	d	p	n	k	l	a	b	l	g	f
k	m	b	p	c	f	a	t	a	b	a	r	y	z
f	i	g	y	o	n	u	z	k	s	r	f	a	s
c	n	n	p	s	l	w	h	e	p	s	j	b	y
p	e	w	e	d	o	q	j	x	i	m	c	n	h
z	o	n	e	c	r	o	c	o	d	i	l	e	k
b	i	r	j	r	t	l	a	s	e	k	v	y	d
v	m	s	p	i	n	e	s	h	r	o	s	g	t

Bonus If a friend's pet needed to disguise itself to avoid danger, what could it do? Explain.

Color Makeover

A chameleon can change colors right before your eyes.

How do chameleons protect themselves and trap tonight's dinner? They change their skin color. Every chameleon has a basic color. This helps it blend into its habitat unseen by its prey. There it can capture an insect or spider with a quick flick of the tongue. Light or temperature differences can trigger a color change. This reptile also changes colors when frightened. How does this happen? A chameleon's skin has many layers. The top layer is easy to see through. The next layer has red and yellow color cells. Then there are layers with blue and white cells. Last is a layer with brown cells. When light, temperature, or mood prompts a change, some color cells get bigger and others get smaller. The size of each cell controls how much color each skin layer displays. Amazingly, a chameleon can make these changes in just a minute!

Complete each sentence by writing five true phrases from the box.

- has a basic color that helps it blend into its surroundings.
- changes color to match its clothes.
- has several layers of skin.
- changes colors when threatened.
- changes color when the air gets colder.
- wears the same colors all the time.
- is a mammal.
- changes color when the light changes.

A chameleon _____

_____

A chameleon _____

_____

A chameleon _____

_____

A chameleon _____

_____

A chameleon _____

_____

Name_____

Color Makeover

Solve each puzzle.
Write the word formed under each puzzle.

1. a lizard known for changing its colors

2. a member of the weasel family whose coat changes to silver-gray in the winter to blend with the snow

3. an insect that hides on dirty tree trunks

4. a bird that can hide in snowbanks because its feathers are white during the winter

5. a twig-like insect that remains still until its prey arrives

6. a mammal whose stripes look like streaks of light and shade in the jungle

7. a slow-moving mammal that can have algae growing on its fur to help it hide in the trees

8. a type of fish that looks like loose gravel on an ocean bed

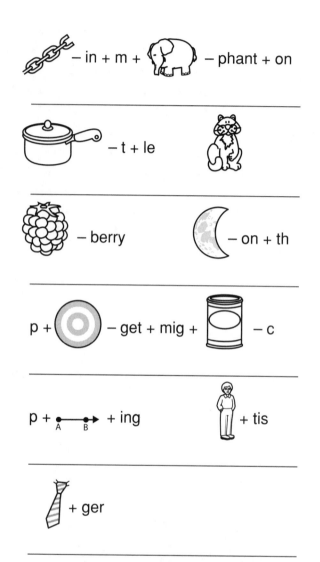

How do humans use protective coloration to protect themselves? Explain.

16   ©The Mailbox® • *Fascinating Facts: Science* • TEC61066 • Key p. 121

Body Shield

The Goliath beetle is called the armored tank of the insect world.

The Goliath beetle is one of the biggest beetles in the world. It can weigh up to 3½ ounces. It can also be up to five inches long. That's one big beetle! A hard, waterproof exoskeleton covers the outside of its body. This covering supports the beetle's body and helps protect the insect from predators. The beetle also has two special front wings that are like leather. They cover and protect the beetle's fragile hind wings. Most Goliath beetles live in the tropical rain forests of Africa. Adult beetles eat sweets, such as fruit and tree sap. As the beetle grows, it molts, or sheds, its outer shell. The beetle must lose this body armor from time to time. Why? It's because the exoskeleton does not grow along with the insect!

Cross out the word that makes each sentence false. Choose a word from the word bank to make the sentence true. Write the new word on the line. Some words will not be used.

1. The Goliath beetle has a soft exoskeleton.

   _____

2. The beetle's front wings help move its hind wings.

   _____

3. The Goliath beetle exercises in order to grow.

   _____

4. The beetle's mother covers and protects it.

   _____

5. Adult Goliath beetles eat fruit and flowers.

   _____

Word Bank

cool	exoskeleton	hard
protect	tree sap	molts
fragile		worms

Name _____

Body Shield

Use the code to spell each animal's name.

Code				
a = 16	e = 3	i = 18	o = 15	u = 9
c = 14	g = 7	l = 10	r = 2	
d = 20	h = 4	m = 12	t = 8	

1. This mollusk's body is covered with a two-part shell that snaps shut when a predator comes near.

14	10	16	12

2. This reptile can pull its head, legs, and tail inside a shell that covers its body.

8	9	2	8	10	3

3. This mammal's upper body is covered with jointed bony plates. It prefers to hide in its burrow when danger is near. When there is no other choice, it will withdraw into its shell.

16	2	12	16	20	18	10	10	15

4. Spines cover the back of this animal to protect it from harm.

4	3	20	7	3	4	15	7

Bonus How might an animal protect itself if it has thick fur rather than a shell? Explain.

18

Dead or Alive?

The opossum can play dead for up to four hours at a time.

For animals, living in the wild involves many factors. They must find food, water, and shelter. Creatures must also be able to protect themselves from danger. The opossum has a unique method of defense. When threatened by a foe, the opossum "plays possum": it goes limp, falls to its side, and enters a comalike state. Its tongue hangs out. Its breathing becomes hard to detect. No amount of nudging can get the opossum going. The opossum also gives off a foul-smelling odor that mimics the stink of a dead animal. This smell scares away predators. The opossum's death act seems real. Well-meaning people sometimes think the opossum is dead and bury it too early. But if left alone, the opossum awakes from its fake death. It escapes unharmed after the danger passes.

Decide whether each sentence is a fact or an opinion. Color the opossum blue if the sentence is a fact. Color the opossum red if the sentence is an opinion.

1. The opossum pretends to be dead to defend itself.

2. This creature gives off the worst odor of any animal.

3. Playing dead is the best way an animal can defend itself.

4. An opossum goes limp when it plays dead.

5. The opossum suffers no harm from playing dead.

6. The most important talent an opossum has is its skill to play dead.

7. After a threat has passed, an opossum can wake up and flee.

8. It is more important for a creature to protect itself than to find food and water.

Name _____

Dead or Alive?

Read each statement below.
Cross out the opossum if the statement is not correct.

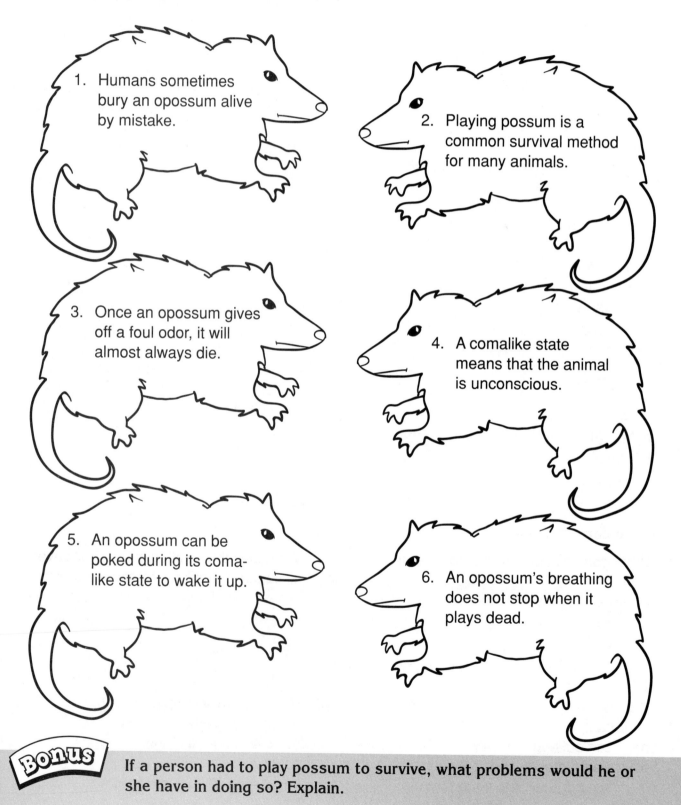

1. Humans sometimes bury an opossum alive by mistake.

2. Playing possum is a common survival method for many animals.

3. Once an opossum gives off a foul odor, it will almost always die.

4. A comalike state means that the animal is unconscious.

5. An opossum can be poked during its comalike state to wake it up.

6. An opossum's breathing does not stop when it plays dead.

Bonus If a person had to play possum to survive, what problems would he or she have in doing so? Explain.

Warning! Stay Away!

A skunk can spray a target from 12 feet away!

What is cute, furry, cat-size, and able to ward off a grown bear with just a wave of its tail? A skunk, of course! It can take only one meeting for many predators to learn to leave this mammal alone. A skunk does not wear its black-and-white coat as camouflage. It is a warning for others to stay away. When attacked, a skunk hisses first. It also growls, stamps its front feet, and raises its tail to caution an attacker. If these tactics fail, the skunk turns around with its tail facing the foe. The two spray glands under its tail are then aimed at the enemy. To defend itself, the small creature sprays the intruder with a foul-smelling liquid. When sprayed near the eyes, the liquid makes it hard for the foe to see. The skunk can escape. The predator is reminded of the meeting for many days. Why? The odor sticks around for a while!

Circle the correct answer.

1. What does a skunk do first to defend itself?
   a. sprays a bad scent
   b. raises its tail
   c. hisses

2. Why is the skunk's black-and-white fur important?
   a. It camouflages the skunk in the wild.
   b. It warns predators to stay away.
   c. It keeps the skunk warm.

3. Why does the skunk aim at a foe's eyes?
   a. to make it difficult for the foe to see
   b. to spray the odor near its mouth
   c. so the foe can see the skunk as it sprays

4. Why does a skunk use its spray on another creature?
   a. to attack
   b. to defend itself
   c. to claim its home area

Warning! Stay Away!

Multiply the row number by the column number.
Write the answer in the correct box.
Then use the code to spell each animal's name.

	1	2	3	4	5	6	7
1	A =	N =	E =	I =	U =	C =	G =
2	N =	I =	C =	P =	B =	L =	H =
3	E =	C =	Z =	L =	R =	T =	M =
4	I =	P =	L =	O =	S =	J =	V =
5	U =	B =	R =	S =	D =	F =	Q =

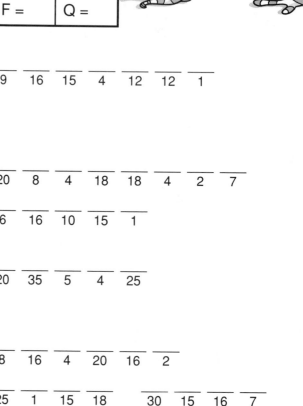

1. This type of polecat has a high-pitched scream. It squirts an attacker with a foul-smelling spray, much like a skunk does.

___ ___ ___ ___ ___ ___ ___
9   16   15   4   12   12   1

2. This snake spits venom in an attacker's eyes. It tilts its head back. Then it uses its fangs to shoot the poison forward.

___ ___ ___ ___ ___ ___ ___ ___
20   8   4   18   18   4   2   7

___ ___ ___ ___ ___
6   16   10   15   1

3. This ocean creature gives off a dark liquid ink to escape an enemy.

___ ___ ___ ___ ___
20   35   5   4   25

4. This brightly colored amphibian is found in Central and South America. Poison comes from its skin. Humans have used this poison on hunting arrows.

___ ___ ___ ___ ___ ___
8   16   4   20   16   2

___ ___ ___ ___   ___ ___ ___ ___
25   1   15   18   30   15   16   7

5. This amphibian sprays a predator with toxins to fend off an attack. Its colors also warn a foe of its poison.

___ ___ ___ ___
30   4   15   3

___ ___ ___ ___ ___ ___ ___ ___ ___ ___
20   1   12   1   21   1   2   25   3   15

Bonus

Do you think an animal that uses a chemical as a defense would use it on its own species? Would it work? Why or why not?

Sensational Swingers

Gibbons can swing at speeds of up to 35 miles per hour to avoid trouble.

No ape wants trouble. This is especially true of the small ape called the gibbon. Gibbons live in the rain forests of Southeast Asia and Indonesia. To help them survive, each close-knit family group lives high off the ground in the rain forest canopy. That's far above where predators, such as leopards and pythons, are usually found. Here, gibbons hunt, eat, sleep, play, and groom themselves. They eat the fruit, buds, and shoots of trees, as well as small animals. Gibbons like to sing to each other. This helps them bond. By singing, they also mark their territory. If they have to flee, these acrobats can be gone in a flash. Their long arms and fingers are just right for swinging. They swing from tree to tree at speeds of up to 35 miles per hour. Still, gibbons are endangered. People hunt them and destroy their homes by cutting down rain forests.

Use the paragraph above to help you answer each question.

1. How do gibbons avoid predators? _____

_____

2. How does singing help the gibbons? _____

_____

3. Why are gibbons endangered? _____

_____

4. What are two animals that are enemies of gibbons? _____

_____

5. How are gibbons like acrobats? _____

_____

Name _____

Sensational Swingers

Read each sentence.
Unscramble the letters to spell the missing word.
Then write the word in the sentence.

1. Gibbons live together in close-knit __ __ __ __ __ groups. (LFMIYA)
                                       3   15

2. Their habitat is the __ __ __ __ __ __ __ __ __ . (IRNA ERFOST)
                        10 12 6   2

3. They eat, sleep, and find food in the tree __ __ __ __ __ __ . (CYPNAO)
                                               4 7   14

4. Their favorite foods include tree fruit, __ __ __ __ , and shoots. (UBSD)
                                            1   16

5. These foods are at the outermost __ __ __ __ __ of the tree canopy. (SEDEG)
                                                11

6. Camouflaged fur helps gibbons __ __ __ __ in trees. (DEIH)
                                  5

7. If threatened, they head for the __ __ __ __ __ __ __ __ . (TPREOSTE)
                                                  8 9

8. Gibbons have few enemies because their homes are so far

   __ __ __ __ __ the ground. (VEOAB)
      13

Complete these sentences by matching letters from the answers above to the numbers below.

9. Gibbons are great arm swingers, or | | | | | | | | | | | | .
                                        1 2 3 4 5 6 7 8 9 10 11

10. They use this ability to | | | | | predators.
                             12 13 14 15 16

Bonus People cut down rain forests to get timber. Suggest how people can get timber without harming the gibbons.

Escape Artists

An impala can run as fast as 50 miles per hour to escape an enemy.

Impalas are midsize antelopes that live alone or in herds of up to 100 impalas. They roam across southern and eastern Africa and live at the edges of grasslands and woodlands. Leopards, wild dogs, and lions all hunt impalas. So do eagles, jackals, and pythons. Therefore, impalas must stay alert. If they sense danger, they explode into action. An impala can jump ten feet into the air, and it runs in a zigzag pattern. Its leaps of up to 30 feet also help protect it from harm. When it raises the hairs on its rump, it warns others of danger. Its speed, along with its quick leaps and jumps, can help the impala escape to safety. In a split second, this graceful animal can be off in a flash!

Read each statement.
Decide whether it is *always, sometimes,* or *never* true.
Then color the correct hoofprint.

	Always	Sometimes	Never
1. Impalas live alone.			
2. Impalas are hunted by a variety of animals.			
3. Impalas leap 30 feet in distance.			
4. Impalas warn others of danger with a loud grunt.			
5. Impalas live at the edge of the woodlands.			

Escape Artists

Read the clues.
Match the prey to its predator.
Then write the correct letter in the blank.

Prey

____ 1. The ostrich has hooflike feet that help it run to safety. Only an enemy that can run faster than the ostrich's 45 miles per hour will catch it.

____ 2. The eastern cottontail rabbit can jump at speeds of up to 18 miles per hour. This helps it escape from an attacker.

____ 3. The skink runs from a foe along the ground. Sometimes the skink breaks away from all or part of its tail to distract the predator while it escapes.

____ 4. An adult giraffe protects itself by kicking and running. The "king of the beasts" is its chief predator.

____ 5. An octopus can squirt water through its body. This allows it to propel itself quickly away from danger.

____ 6. The African zebra can make a dash to get away from an enemy. Its stripes also help it hide from foes.

Predator

A. The lion preys on some of the larger animals of the African landscape. Hunting with a group improves the lion's chances of capturing its prey.

B. The hyena lives in Africa. It uses its sharp eyesight to spot its prey's distinct stripes.

C. The moray eel will eat about any kind of fish or mollusk. If its prey is too large, the eel will tear it into smaller pieces to eat.

D. The coyote used to live in western North America but now roams much of the continent. It prefers to eat small furry mammals.

E. The crow is not a picky eater. It will search along the ground for insects, nuts, grains, and worms to eat.

F. The cheetah is the fastest short-distance runner on land. It can run up to 70 miles per hour to capture its next meal.

Bonus Which of the five senses do you think would be most helpful to an animal that uses escape as a defense? Explain.

Name _____

Hide-and-Seek

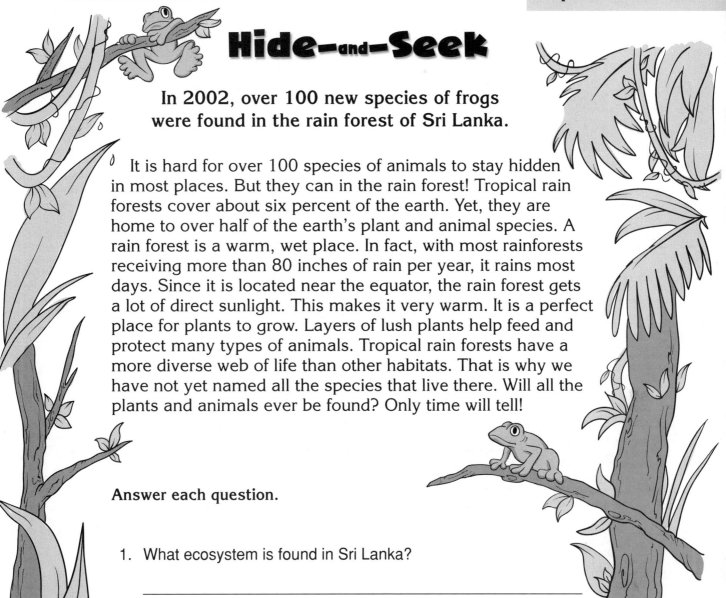

In 2002, over 100 new species of frogs were found in the rain forest of Sri Lanka.

It is hard for over 100 species of animals to stay hidden in most places. But they can in the rain forest! Tropical rain forests cover about six percent of the earth. Yet, they are home to over half of the earth's plant and animal species. A rain forest is a warm, wet place. In fact, with most rainforests receiving more than 80 inches of rain per year, it rains most days. Since it is located near the equator, the rain forest gets a lot of direct sunlight. This makes it very warm. It is a perfect place for plants to grow. Layers of lush plants help feed and protect many types of animals. Tropical rain forests have a more diverse web of life than other habitats. That is why we have not yet named all the species that live there. Will all the plants and animals ever be found? Only time will tell!

Answer each question.

1. What ecosystem is found in Sri Lanka?

   _____

2. Why do so many types of animals live in the rain forest?

   _____

   _____

3. How is the rain forest different from other habitats?

   _____

4. Do you think scientists will ever find and name all species?

   Explain. _____

   _____

Hide-and-Seek

Match the numbers to the letters in the code.
If your answers are correct, you will spell the names of some animals that live in the rain forest.

CODE	
A	2
B	11
C	21
D	12
E	3
F	20
G	7
H	19
I	1
J	22
K	13
L	10
M	18
N	16
O	4
R	8
S	6
T	9
U	5
W	15
Y	17

1. | 19 | 4 | 15 | 10 | 3 | 8 | | 18 | 4 | 16 | 13 | 3 | 17 |

2. | 9 | 4 | 5 | 21 | 2 | 16 |

3. | 9 | 2 | 18 | 2 | 16 | 12 | 5 | 2 |

4. | 9 | 8 | 3 | 3 | | 11 | 4 | 2 | | 21 | 4 | 16 | 6 | 9 | 8 | 1 | 21 | 9 | 4 | 8 |

5. | 22 | 2 | 7 | 5 | 2 | 8 |

6. | 10 | 3 | 2 | 20 | | 21 | 5 | 9 | 9 | 3 | 8 | | 2 | 16 | 9 |
   with a dash (-) in one of the lower boxes.

Bonus

The four main layers of the rain forest from top to bottom are the canopy, the sub-canopy, the understory, and the floor. Which layer(s) do you think each of the following animals call home: spider monkey, macaw, iguana? Explain.

Name_____

LEAFY FACTS

Some deciduous trees are great recyclers! They reuse a key substance that allows them to survive season after season.

In summer, broad-leaved trees are green and lush. Their leaves are full of green chlorophyll. But in the fall, some deciduous trees take this green substance back from their leaves and store it until spring returns. Without chlorophyll, the leaves look red, yellow, or orange. Soon, the autumn leaves die and fall from the branches. Without green leaves, trees stop making food, and photosynthesis ends. Months pass. When spring arrives, the days get warmer. Then the trees send the stored chlorophyll to the leaf sprouts. New leaves grow. Days lengthen, and the forest turns green. But this does not last forever. In time, the season changes again. The days grow shorter, and the temperature drops once more. These changes signal to the forest that it's time to recycle again through yet another cold winter.

Circle the correct answer.

1. Why does the passage call some deciduous trees great recyclers?
   a. Deciduous trees are green and lush.
   b. They store chlorophyll to use again after winter.
   c. They use the same leaves over and over.

2. How does losing leaves help a tree survive in winter?
   a. The tree does not have to use its energy to feed the leaves.
   b. The tree has less weight to hold.
   c. Photosynthesis can begin without the leaves.

3. What makes the new leaves green in the spring?
   a. The temperature falls.
   b. There is less rain and sunlight.
   c. Chlorophyll returns to the leaves.

4. What is one way that a deciduous tree prepares for winter?
   a. It sheds leaves.
   b. Its leaves turn green.
   c. Its roots stop taking in water and minerals.

LEAFY FACTS

Complete each sentence with a word from the
   word bank.
Then number the leaves in the order in which
   the events occur.
The first leaf has been numbered for you.

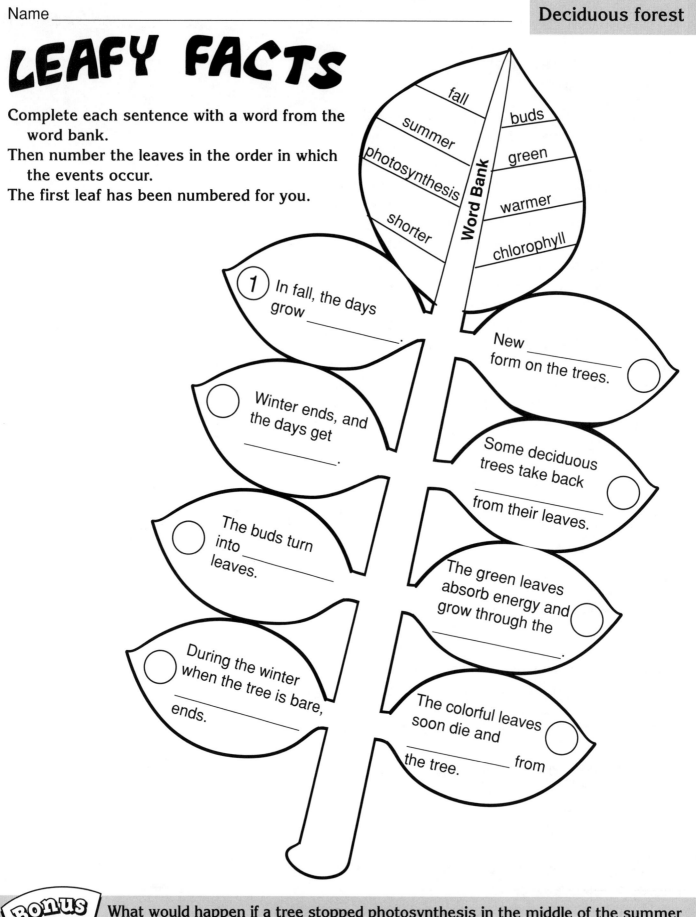

Word Bank

fall
summer
photosynthesis
shorter
buds
green
warmer
chlorophyll

1   In fall, the days grow _____ .

New _____ form on the trees.

Winter ends, and the days get _____ .

Some deciduous trees take back _____ from their leaves.

The buds turn into _____ leaves.

The green leaves absorb energy and grow through the _____ .

During the winter when the tree is bare, _____ ends.

The colorful leaves soon die and _____ from the tree.

Bonus   What would happen if a tree stopped photosynthesis in the middle of the summer and lost all of its leaves? What would happen the next spring? Explain.

A Sea of Grass

Grasslands cover about one-fourth of the earth's land.

Prairies, savannas, and steppes are all grasslands. All are large, flat lands where grasses grow well. Many animals depend on these places. People depend on them too. That's because grasslands provide most of the world's food. Wheat and corn are grasses that grow in the rich soil.

Grasslands have three to four layers. The top layer, called humus, is the most fertile. Here, rotting plants and animals enrich the soil. The second layer is topsoil. Plants often spread their roots in the topsoil. Rain and heat help soak minerals from the top layer to this layer. Subsoil is the third layer. During the wet season, this layer stores water. During the dry season, the stored water rises to the topsoil. This can help plants survive a drought. Some grasslands also have a fourth layer of solid rock. The number of layers may differ, but all grasslands have special value. They feed the world!

Color the correct stalk of wheat to show whether each sentence is true or false.

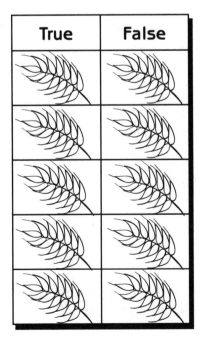

True	False

1. All grasslands have a layer of rock.

2. The richest part of the soil is called humus.

3. The grasslands have fertile soil in which we can grow food.

4. All of the earth's food supply comes from the grasslands.

5. A decaying animal body enriches the soil.

Name _____

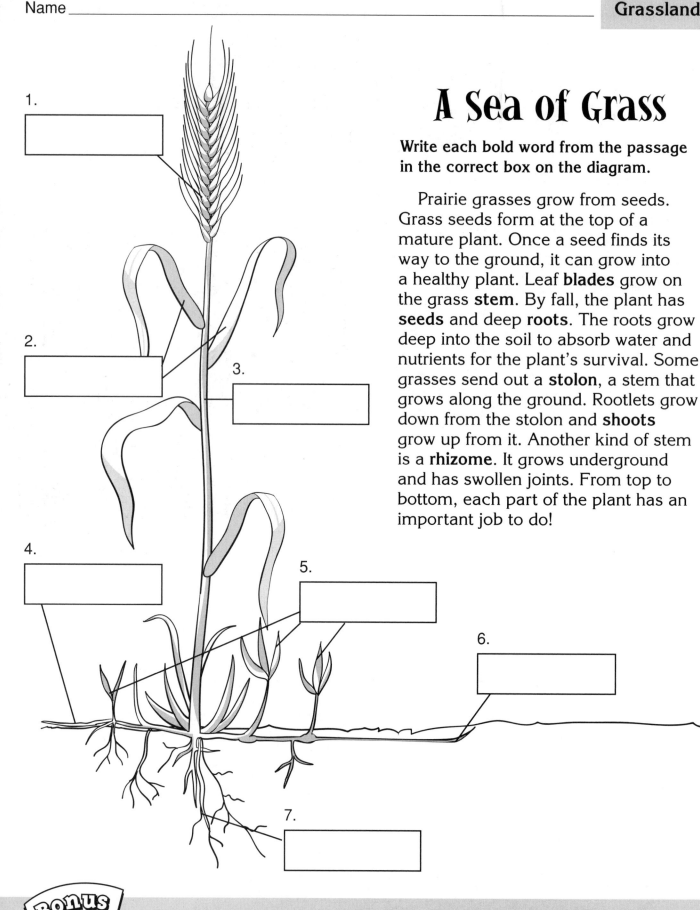

1.

2.

3.

4.

5.

6.

7.

A Sea of Grass

Write each bold word from the passage in the correct box on the diagram.

Prairie grasses grow from seeds. Grass seeds form at the top of a mature plant. Once a seed finds its way to the ground, it can grow into a healthy plant. Leaf **blades** grow on the grass **stem**. By fall, the plant has **seeds** and deep **roots**. The roots grow deep into the soil to absorb water and nutrients for the plant's survival. Some grasses send out a **stolon**, a stem that grows along the ground. Rootlets grow down from the stolon and **shoots** grow up from it. Another kind of stem is a **rhizome**. It grows underground and has swollen joints. From top to bottom, each part of the plant has an important job to do!

Bonus

What might happen if the grasslands vanished from the earth? Explain.

Harsh Habitat

Most deserts receive less than ten inches of rain a year!

Deserts can be hot during the day and cold at night, but they are always dry. Wind and sand cause erosion to occur in these arid lands. A desert sandstorm can last for days! Dunes are often moved or reshaped. Sometimes sand even covers roads. Water is scarce in a desert. But adaptations help many animals survive desert life. Some creatures estivate, or become inactive, when it's too hot. Others get water from the plants they eat. Plants can use long roots to get water from deep underground. Some plants and animals are lucky enough to live in an oasis. Water is found there in wells and springs. But oases are few and far between. Since about one-third of the earth's land is desert, it's great that so many species have found ways to survive there.

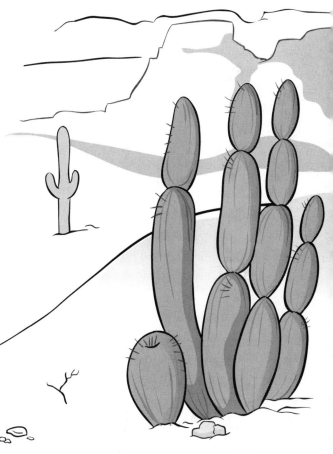

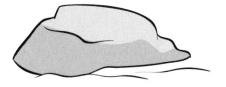

**Find a word in the passage for each definition.
Then write the word in the blank.**

Glossary

1. _____: adjustments that help animals survive in a certain setting

2. _____: very dry; too dry to raise crops

3. _____: a fierce windstorm that can cover roads with sand

4. _____: to become inactive during hot weather

5. _____: a fertile place in the desert where water can be found

Harsh Habitat

Unscramble the words to complete each headline.

ECOSYSTEM EXAMINER

SPECIAL ISSUE
DESERT ADAPTATIONS

1. Scorpions Never _____ (rikDn)!

2. Desert Kangaroo Rat Seals _____ (rruwoB) to Trap Moisture From Exhaled Air

3. A Saguaro _____ (tusCca) Can Weigh Six Tons Because It Holds a Lot of Water!

NEWS FLASH

4. Hair on _____ (eetF) of Fennec Fox Allows It to Run on Hot Sand!

5. Camels Survive off Fat in _____ (mpHus) When Food Is Scarce!

6. Thorny Devil Covers Self With Soil at Night to Stay _____ (arWm) and Burrows Underground During Day to Stay Cool

7. Male Sandgrouse Soaks Up Water Through Belly _____ (heaetrFs) for Its Chicks!

Bonus

What are three ways that plants could adapt to survive in the desert?

Life on the Tundra

Permafrost is a layer of frozen soil that never melts. It can be 3,000 feet deep!

No biome changes as much as the tundra. Winter brings months of darkness to this white land. Many plants are dormant during the winter. Since food is scarce here, many animals migrate to warmer lands. But that all changes in spring and summer when the hours of daylight increase. In the summer, the sun never sets. Insects begin to buzz and animals return to feed and have babies. Some creatures even change color. Brown fur becomes a better color for camouflage than white. Inactive plants become active again. New plants spread shallow roots near the earth's surface. But large plants cannot survive here, even in the summer. This is because their roots cannot break through the permafrost. In time, the hours of daylight decrease. The cold creeps back in. The tundra turns white once more, and the cycle repeats itself. Welcome to the land of extreme seasonal changes!

Complete the chart to compare and contrast the tundra's seasons.

	Spring/Summer	**Fall/Winter**
Sunlight		
Temperature		
Plants		
Animals		

Name _____

Life on the Tundra

Use the word bank to spell the names of creatures that live on the tundra in the times shown.

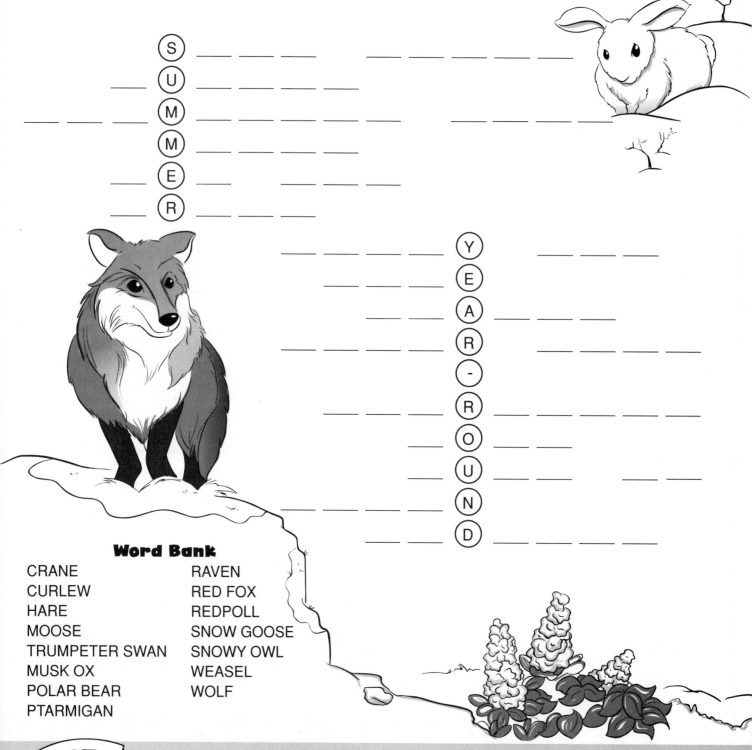

S _____ _____ _____ _____ _____ _____
_____ U _____ _____ _____ _____
_____ _____ _____ M _____ _____ _____
_____ M _____ _____ _____ _____
_____ E _____ _____
_____ _____ R _____

_____ _____ _____ _____ Y _____ _____ _____ _____
_____ _____ _____ E _____ _____
_____ _____ A _____
_____ _____ _____ R _____ _____
-
_____ _____ R _____ _____
_____ O _____ _____
_____ _____ U _____
_____ N _____
D _____ _____

Word Bank

CRANE   RAVEN
CURLEW   RED FOX
HARE   REDPOLL
MOOSE   SNOW GOOSE
TRUMPETER SWAN   SNOWY OWL
MUSK OX   WEASEL
POLAR BEAR   WOLF
PTARMIGAN

Bonus Research one of the animals that lives on the tundra year-round. How does that animal adapt to survive in this region?

To the Taiga

Pinecones are either male or female.

Between the tundra and the deciduous forest lies a sea of green called the taiga. In the taiga, it is below freezing for more than half of the year. Its growing season is short. But cone-bearing trees called conifers help the taiga stay green. Spruce, fir, and pine trees are all conifers. These trees have needlelike leaves and downward-sloping branches. The trees' angled branches let snow slide off easily. Most conifers do not lose their leaves in the fall. Some even keep them for 15 years! A waxy coating on the leaves helps hold in water. Both male and female cones are on most conifers. The female cone is large and bears seeds. The smaller male cone scatters pollen and then withers and dies. Even though the taiga is frost-free for only a few months of the year, it is green all year long thanks to the trees!

Use the passage to answer the questions.

1. Why is the taiga green? _____

_____

2. Describe a conifer tree. _____

_____

3. How are the male cone and the female cone different? Explain. _____

_____

_____

4. Describe the taiga's climate. _____

_____

To the Taiga

The shaded area of the map shows the taiga region.
Read the clues.
Then color the boxes on the map by the code.

Color Code
blue   = lake
red   = park
green = mountain

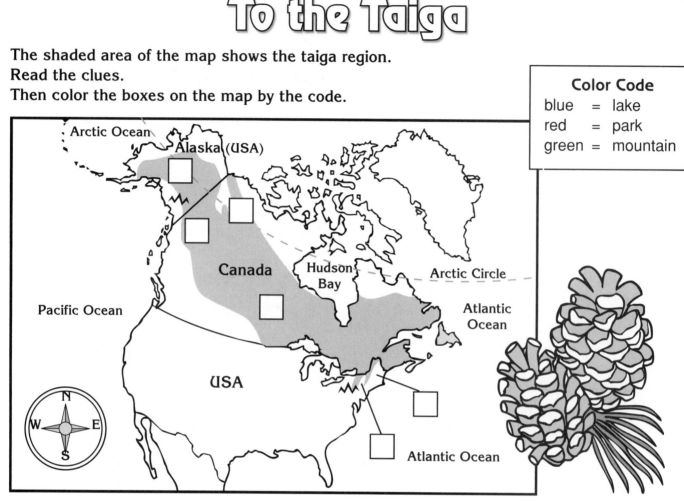

Clues

 Great Bear Lake lies near the northern edge of Canada's taiga. A part of the lake lies in the Arctic Circle.

 Denali National Park in western Alaska includes Mt. McKinley and is the home of the world's second largest taiga reserve.

 Another area of taiga is in the Adirondack Mountains in the northeast part of New York.

 One more part of the taiga in the United States is found in Acadia National Park in Maine. The red crossbill, a small bird, feeds on the seeds of the park's cone-bearing trees.

 The Yukon Territory to the east of Alaska is the site of the highest mountain in Canada. This area has the typical land and climate of the taiga.

 Grasslands surround the taiga in Riding Mountain National Park in south-central Canada.

Bonus

Why do you think that Canada has more taiga than the United States? Explain.

Name _____

THE CORAL KINGDOM

Coral reefs build slowly. It takes a whole year or longer for five inches of reef to form!

A coral reef is made of the skeletons of tiny sea creatures. Yet, it is full of life. Many fish swim around the reef. But it is each coral polyp, also known as the stony coral, that is vital here. Coral polyps are tiny animals with tube-shaped bodies. Their flowing tentacles help them catch food. Stony corals are important because the outer skeletons they form help build reefs. Most corals live in colonies in warm, shallow saltwater. Corals need sunlight to live. When alive, they are food for other creatures. But when they die, their soft bodies decay, leaving behind hard skeletons. Over time, this graveyard of coral polyps begins to form a reef. Plants and animals move in as more tiny remains help the reef keep growing. A few reefs are so large that they can be seen from space!

Mark out the word that makes each sentence false.
Then write a new word in its place to make the sentence true.

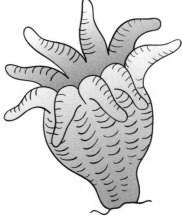

1. Coral polyps live in cold, shallow saltwater.

2. Coral reefs are made of the skeletons of soft coral.

3. The bodies of large stony corals build a reef over time.

4. Coral reefs grow quickly.

5. When coral polyps die, they leave behind soft skeletons.

6. Coral polyps have cone-shaped bodies.

THE CORAL KINGDOM

Read each clue. Then use the words in the word bank to write the name of the matching creature in the puzzle. Some words will not be used.

1. I use small suckers on my arms to move slowly across the reef.

2. If I get my eight arms around my prey, it will be in trouble!

3. I have a pouch like a kangaroo and a head like a horse.

4. I live in the empty shell of a snail. I crawl in when the snail moves out.

5. I am a feared meat-eating fish.

6. I am named after a part of the human body.

7. I am also called a devilfish because of the cranky way I behave.

8. I molt and grow a new shell many times during my life.

9. I am quite colorful. I get my name from a flower.

Where is the Great Barrier Reef, which is over 1,200 miles long?

To find out, copy the letters in the bold boxes in order from top to bottom. Begin your answer with a capital letter.

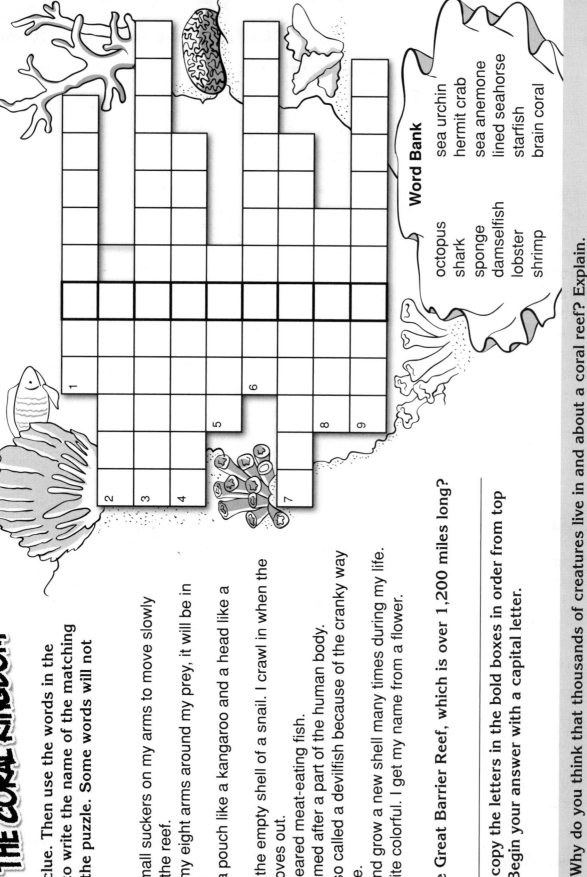

Word Bank

octopus	sea urchin
shark	hermit crab
sponge	sea anemone
damselfish	lined seahorse
lobster	starfish
shrimp	brain coral

BONUS Why do you think that thousands of creatures live in and about a coral reef? Explain.

The Air Above

Our planet is covered with four blankets of air.

The earth's atmosphere has four major layers. Gravity holds them in place. Each layer helps keep the earth safe. Scientists study all the layers. The layer closest to the earth contains gases that support life. Weather watchers study what goes on in this layer to make forecasts. The second layer above the earth contains the ozone layer. Ozone is a gas that blocks harmful rays from the sun. In the third layer of air, meteors are burned up. This keeps most meteors from reaching the surface of the earth. The fourth layer of air reflects radio waves back to Earth. That allows people to communicate by radio. We should feel pretty safe with all this help!

Thermosphere

Use ideas from the passage and drawing to complete each sentence.

1. Because the earth has gravity, the earth's atmosphere _____ _____ .

Mesosphere

2. Since scientists study changes that occur in the first layer, _____ _____ .

3. If a meteor enters the third layer of the earth's atmosphere, it will most likely be _____ .

Stratosphere

4. We can stay in touch with people all over the world because the fourth layer of air _____ _____ .

5. If we did not have the second layer of air, _____   Troposphere
_____
_____ .

The Air Above

Use the code to name each instrument and the atmospheric condition it measures.

1. A __ __ __ __ __ __ __ __ __ __
   1 10 13 4 5 19 2 18 2 4
   measures
   __ __ __ __ __ __ __ __ .
   1 7 19 9 15 9 18 10

2. A __ __ __ __ __ __ __ __ __
   3 11 4 5 19 2 18 2 4
   measures
   __ __ __ __ __ __ __ __ __ __ __ .
   11 9 4   6 4 2 16 16 7 4 2

3. A __ __ __ __ __ __ __ __ __
   4 11 9 14   13 11 7 13 2
   measures
   __ __ __ __ __ __ __ __ __ __ __ __ __ .
   6 4 2 12 9 6 9 18 11 18 9 5 14

4. A __ __ __ __ __ __ __ __ __ __ __
   18 1 2 4 19 5 19 2 18 2 4
   measures
   __ __ __ __ __ __ __ __ __ __ __ .
   18 2 19 6 2 4 11 18 7 4 2

5. A __ __ __ __ __ __ __ __
   8 9 14 15   17 11 14 2
   measures
   __ __ __ __ __ __ __ __ __ __ __ __ __ .
   8 9 14 15   15 9 4 2 12 18 9 5 14

6. An __ __ __ __ __ __ __ __ __ __ __
   11 14 2 19 5 19 2 18 2 4
   measures
   __ __ __ __ __ __ __ __ __ .
   8 9 14 15   16 6 2 2 15

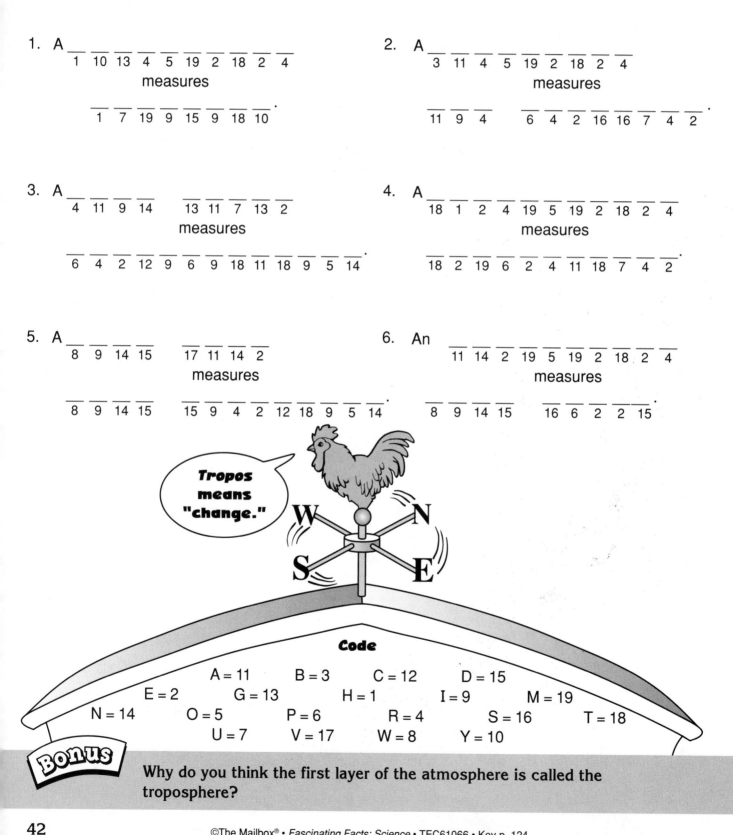

Tropos means "change."

W   N
S   E

Code

A = 11   B = 3   C = 12   D = 15
E = 2   G = 13   H = 1   I = 9   M = 19
N = 14   O = 5   P = 6   R = 4   S = 16   T = 18
U = 7   V = 17   W = 8   Y = 10

Bonus

Why do you think the first layer of the atmosphere is called the troposphere?

Vital Vapors

If you've ever gone through fog, you've been in a low cloud.

How do clouds form? They form when cool air mixes with water vapor. Water vapor is a gas that forms when water from oceans, lakes, rivers, and ponds evaporates. Water vapor also comes from water on plants and in damp soil. The amount of water vapor the air can hold depends on how hot or cold the air is. Warmer air holds more water vapor than cooler air. When warm air rises, it cools. The cooled water vapor changes into a liquid and mixes with dust in the air. Then water droplets are formed. There are millions of water droplets in a cloud. There are also many kinds of clouds. The type of cloud formed depends on the weather and height at which the water vapor condenses. A cloud that is close to the ground is called fog. What's your favorite type of cloud?

Answer the questions.

1. What is water vapor? _____

   _____

2. Which type of air can hold more water vapor: warm air or cool air? _____

3. What happens when water vapor cools? _____

   _____

4. How is fog different from other types of clouds? _____

   _____

5. What factors determine the types of clouds that form? _____

   _____

Name _____

Vital Vapors

Circle the correct answers. Use the chart for help.

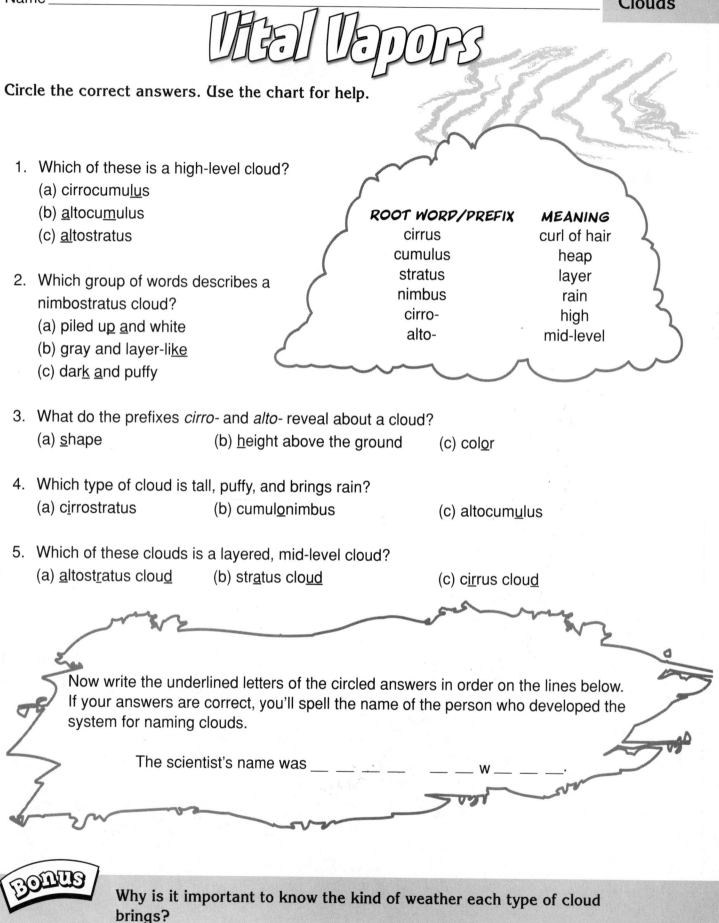

ROOT WORD/PREFIX	MEANING
cirrus	curl of hair
cumulus	heap
stratus	layer
nimbus	rain
cirro-	high
alto-	mid-level

1. Which of these is a high-level cloud?
   (a) cirrocumu<u>l</u>us
   (b) <u>a</u>ltocumulus
   (c) <u>a</u>ltostratus

2. Which group of words describes a nimbostratus cloud?
   (a) piled u<u>p</u> <u>a</u>nd white
   (b) gray and layer-li<u>ke</u>
   (c) dar<u>k</u> <u>a</u>nd puffy

3. What do the prefixes *cirro-* and *alto-* reveal about a cloud?
   (a) <u>s</u>hape   (b) <u>h</u>eight above the ground   (c) col<u>o</u>r

4. Which type of cloud is tall, puffy, and brings rain?
   (a) c<u>i</u>rrostratus   (b) cumul<u>o</u>nimbus   (c) altocumu<u>l</u>us

5. Which of these clouds is a layered, mid-level cloud?
   (a) <u>a</u>ltost<u>r</u>atus clou<u>d</u>   (b) str<u>a</u>tus clo<u>ud</u>   (c) c<u>i</u>rrus cloud

Now write the underlined letters of the circled answers in order on the lines below. If your answers are correct, you'll spell the name of the person who developed the system for naming clouds.

The scientist's name was __ __ __ __   __ __ w __ __ __.

Bonus

Why is it important to know the kind of weather each type of cloud brings?

The Sky Is Falling!

Most hailstones are the size of peas. One that fell in Kansas was as big as a grapefruit.

Rain, snow, sleet, and hail are types of precipitation. Each one is a form of water that falls from the sky. The kind of precipitation that falls depends upon how warm or cold the air is. It rains when water droplets in a cloud join and fall. If a cloud is cold, the water droplets form tiny ice crystals. When the crystals collide, they form snowflakes. Snowflakes that fall through warm air melt and turn to rain. If raindrops or melted snow crystals fall through freezing air, they turn into small balls of ice called sleet. Hailstones are frozen raindrops that grow into lumps of ice in a thunderstorm cloud. Sometimes air currents take hailstones through water droplets that do not freeze even though the temperature is below freezing. When this happens, the hailstones get bigger. All forms of precipitation are helpful because they return water to the earth!

Write a word from the word bank to complete each sentence. One word will not be used.

Word Bank
brighter
freeze
cold
warm
water
larger

1. All forms of precipitation return _____ to the earth.

2. Rain occurs when drops of water fall through _____ air.

3. When raindrops fall through cold air and _____, sleet forms.

4. Snow occurs when ice crystals form inside clouds and fall through

   _____ air.

5. Hailstones can get _____ during a hailstorm.

The Sky Is Falling!

Write the correct word to complete each sentence.
Then circle each answer in the puzzle.

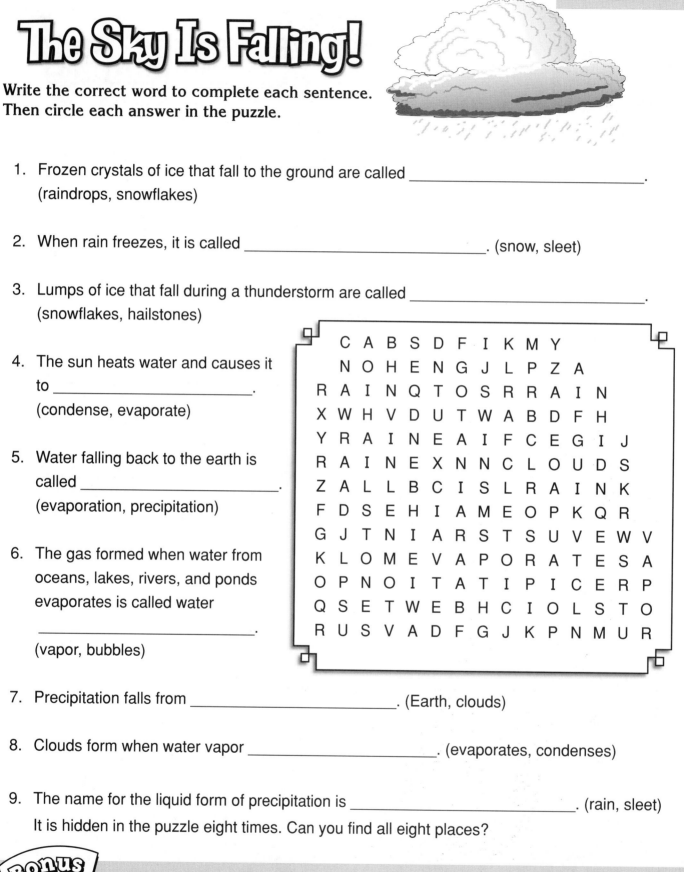

1. Frozen crystals of ice that fall to the ground are called _____.
    (raindrops, snowflakes)

2. When rain freezes, it is called _____. (snow, sleet)

3. Lumps of ice that fall during a thunderstorm are called _____.
    (snowflakes, hailstones)

4. The sun heats water and causes it
    to _____.
    (condense, evaporate)

5. Water falling back to the earth is
    called _____.
    (evaporation, precipitation)

6. The gas formed when water from
    oceans, lakes, rivers, and ponds
    evaporates is called water
    _____.
    (vapor, bubbles)

```
C A B S D F I K M Y
N O H E N G J L P Z A
R A I N Q T O S R R A I N
X W H V D U T W A B D F H
Y R A I N E A I F C E G I J
R A I N E X N N C L O U D S
Z A L L B C I S L R A I N K
F D S E H I A M E O P K Q R
G J T N I A R S T S U V E W V
K L O M E V A P O R A T E S A
O P N O I T A T I P I C E R P
Q S E T W E B H C I O L S T O
R U S V A D F G J K P N M U R
```

7. Precipitation falls from _____. (Earth, clouds)

8. Clouds form when water vapor _____. (evaporates, condenses)

9. The name for the liquid form of precipitation is _____. (rain, sleet)
    It is hidden in the puzzle eight times. Can you find all eight places?

Bonus

**All living things need water to survive. Rain provides water. What
happens when there is too much or too little water?**

©The Mailbox® • *Fascinating Facts: Science* • TEC61066 • Key p. 124

NATURAL BREEZES

The crew on sailing ships sometimes threw horses overboard to conserve water when weak winds couldn't move the ships.

Wind is moving air. Some winds are strong. Others are gentle. Winds blow because some places on the earth get more heat from the sun than others. This uneven heating causes the air to move. As warm air rises, cool air rushes in to take its place. The air moves from high pressure to low pressure. Winds are stronger when there is a great difference in the pressure. Winds that occur in one place—such as mountains, valleys, or coastal regions—are called local winds. Steady winds also blow over large sections of the earth. These sections have special names, such as the horse latitudes. Sailing ships often got stranded in the horse latitudes because the wind there was not strong enough to move a ship. Sailors soon learned to use the more reliable trade winds. Winds are named by the direction from which they blow. So an easterly blows from east to west!

Prevailing Winds

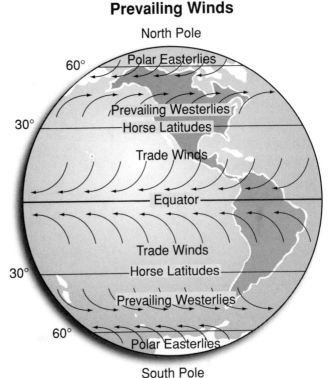

Write "T" or "F" to tell whether each sentence is true or false.

_____ 1. An easterly blows from west to east.

_____ 2. When the difference in air pressure is great, winds are weak.

_____ 3. The best winds for sailing ships to use are the horse latitudes.

_____ 4. Winds blow from high pressure to low pressure.

_____ 5. Winds blow because of the even heating of the earth.

NATURAL BREEZES

Read the text for each diagram.
Then cut out the boxes at the bottom of the page and glue them to the matching diagrams.

1.

> Glue diagram title here.

When days are sunny, the land heats up faster than the sea. The warm air above the land rises. Cooler air from over the sea moves in to replace it. This causes a sea breeze.

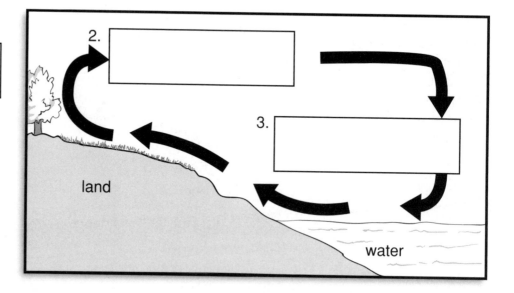

2.

3.

land

water

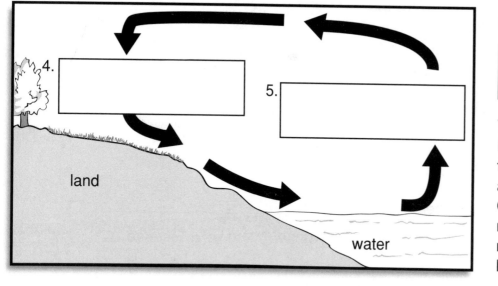

4.

5.

land

water

6.

> Glue diagram title here.

When the sun sets, the land cools off faster than the sea. The warm air above the sea rises. Cooler air from the land moves toward the sea to replace it. This causes a land breeze.

Bonus How is wind helpful? How is it harmful?

| warm air rising | cool air sinking | **Sea Breeze** |
| warm air rising | cool air sinking | **Land Breeze** |

48

Name _____

CLUES TO CLIMATE

The remains of old trees tell us what the climate was like 8,000 years ago.

Climate is the average of all weather over a length of time. Temperature and precipitation are the most important factors of climate. Wind direction and speed also are factors. Records about climates have been kept for about 150 years. So what was the earth's climate like before that? To find out, scientists look for clues. Tree rings, fossils, and ships' logs all hold hints about the past. Scientists have not found enough clues to know all the answers. But they do know that the climate is always changing. Over time, more clues will be found. Those clues might help us adapt to future climate changes!

Write the correct answer in the blank.

1. _____ is not a major factor of climate.

    a. temperature   b. a ship's diary   c. wind direction

2. Records about climates have been kept for less than _____.

    a. two centuries   b. two decades   c. two years

3. *Climate* is the _____ of weather over time.

    a. daily record   b. average   c. weekly study

4. Scientists have used _____ to learn about climates.

    a. fossils   b. written records   c. fossils and written records

CLUES TO CLIMATE

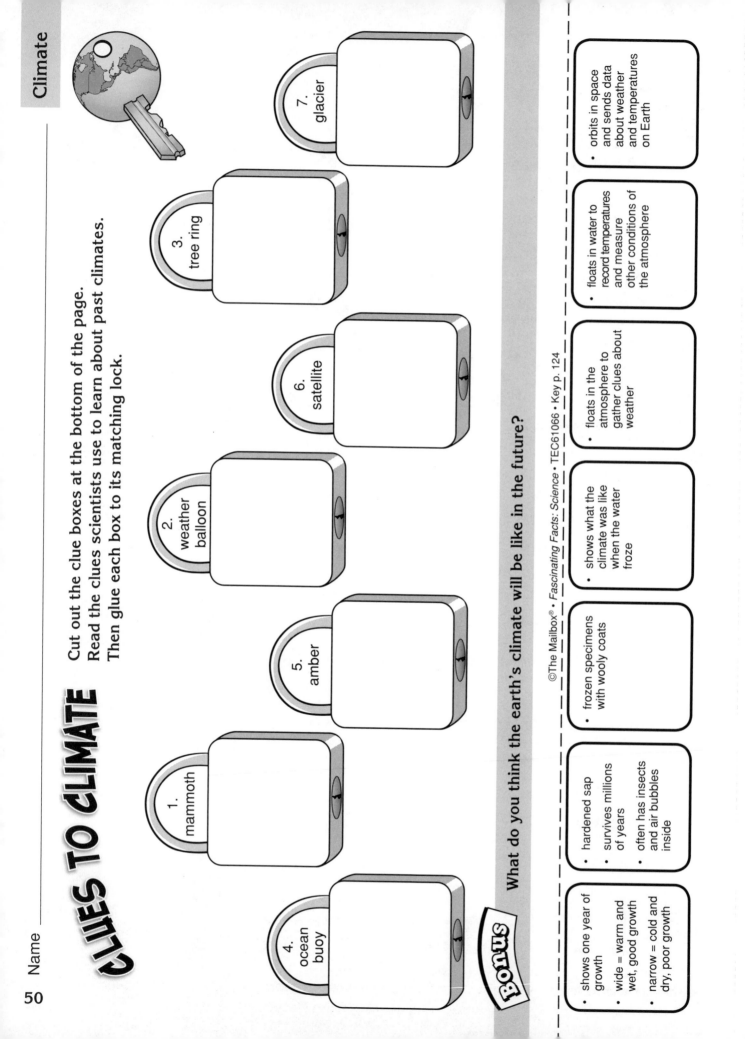

Cut out the clue boxes at the bottom of the page.
Read the clues scientists use to learn about past climates.
Then glue each box to its matching lock.

1. mammoth

2. weather balloon

3. tree ring

4. ocean buoy

5. amber

6. satellite

7. glacier

What do you think the earth's climate will be like in the future?

Bonus

©The Mailbox® • Fascinating Facts: Science • TEC61066 • Key p. 124

- orbits in space and sends data about weather and temperatures on Earth

- floats in water to record temperatures and measure other conditions of the atmosphere

- floats in the atmosphere to gather clues about weather

- shows what the climate was like when the water froze

- frozen specimens with wooly coats

- hardened sap
- survives millions of years
- often has insects and air bubbles inside

- shows one year of growth
- wide = warm and wet, good growth
- narrow = cold and dry, poor growth

Spiraling Sea Storms

On average, ten tropical storms form in the Atlantic Ocean each year. About six of these storms become hurricanes.

When a hurricane is forecast, it's time to get serious. A **hurricane** is a monster storm that packs winds of at least 74 miles per hour. It starts as a cluster of thunderstorms over warm waters near the **equator.** A weather system like this can then strengthen into a **tropical depression.** If weather conditions are just right, a tropical depression can become a **tropical storm.** If a tropical storm grows stronger, it can turn into a hurricane. It's often too late to think about what to do once a hurricane arrives. So scientists study tropical depressions using satellites in space and other means. They watch for signs that a storm is getting stronger. If it does, the weather watchers warn people in its path about the coming wind, rain, and high seas!

Label the diagram using the bold words from the passage.

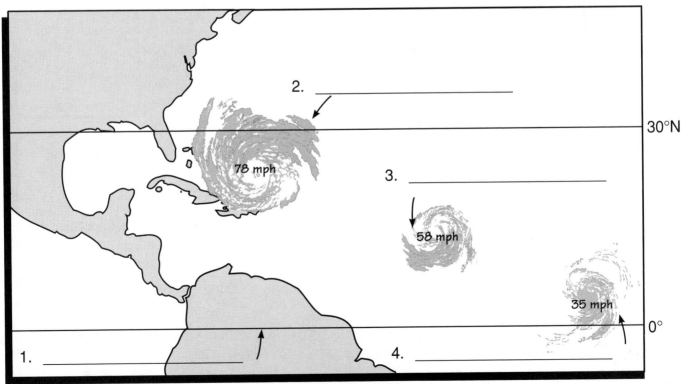

2. _____

30°N

3. _____

78 mph

58 mph

35 mph

0°

1. _____

4. _____

Spiraling Sea Storms

Unscramble each word to complete each hurricane hazard.

1. A storm _____ (usrge) is a dome of water more than 15 feet deep and up to 100 miles wide. It hits the coast close to where a hurricane comes onto land.

2. Most of the time, stronger storms mean more wind _____ (amadge) to homes and property.

3. Six to 12 _____ (esnchi) of rain can fall when a hurricane moves through an area.

4. Heavy rain from a hurricane can cause _____ (olodfngi).

5. A hurricane can also cause tornadoes to form _____ (ndarou) its edges.

6. The _____ (engsttrh) of a hurricane depends on its wind speed.

7. Hurricane winds blow at speeds of 74 miles per hour and more. The force can _____ (estdroy) buildings.

8. Loose items such as lawn chairs can be picked up by strong _____ (inwds) and thrown through the air.

9. Hurricane winds can take down _____ (seter).

10. Very strong winds arrive _____ (febroe) the hurricane eye moves over land.

Now unscramble the underlined letters to find out what is in the outer bands of a hurricane. Some of the letters have been placed for you.

t __ __ __ __ e __ s __ __ __ m __

Bonus

Why are places with large numbers of people living there at a greater risk during a hurricane than places with fewer people?

Just Passing Through

A tornado can pick up cows, cars, and people.

Iowa and Oklahoma are not neighbors. But they have something in common with eight other states. All are part of a stretch of land in the center of the United States known as Tornado Alley. More twisters occur here than anywhere else in the world. A tornado is a swirling column of air that forms and often goes away quickly. Its winds can reach 300 miles per hour and smash buildings to bits. Sometimes people are killed. Most tornadoes form during thunderstorms. Scientists observe tornado damage and then use a special scale to tell how strong or weak the tornado was. Some tornadoes are strong enough to lift cars and homes in the air. There are even stories of humans and animals being picked up and set down unharmed. But gentleness is not what these strong storms are known for. Just ask the people in Tornado Alley!

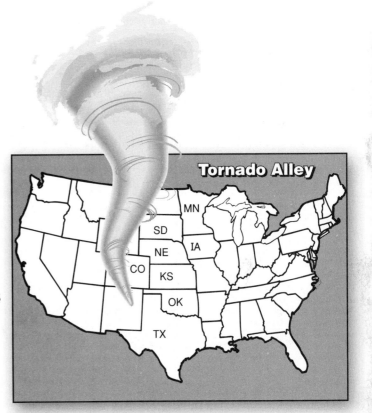

Tornado Alley

Write "sometimes," "always," or "never" to answer each question.

_____ 1. Tornadoes occur in places other than Tornado Alley.

_____ 2. Winds in a tornado reach speeds greater than 500 miles per hour.

_____ 3. Tornadoes form and then vanish.

_____ 4. Tornadoes are deadly.

_____ 5. Scientists can only guess about a tornado's strength based on the damage it does.

Name _____

Just Passing Through

Decide whether each statement is a fact or an opinion.
Color the matching funnel cloud to show your answer.

FACT	OPINION	
W	K	1. Few tornadoes last more than a few minutes.
A	I	2. Twisters can snap trees, twist metal, and topple trains.
H	S	3. I think that people should learn what to do during a tornado.
H	A	4. Most people who take shelter survive a tornado.
I	M	5. Tornadoes can travel 60 miles per hour.
N	L	6. Drivers who try to drive faster than a tornado can be killed or injured.
O	G	7. Staying in a mobile home during a tornado is probably a bad idea.
Y	T	8. I believe that tornadoes are the worst storms of all.
O	T	9. Most tornadoes are small.
N	C	10. Damage costs from tornadoes can be millions of dollars.

Write the letters of the uncolored funnel clouds above on the matching numbered lines below.
If your answers are correct, you will spell the name of a city that is often hit by tornadoes
   because it is so near the heart of Tornado Alley.

___ ___ ___ ___ ___ ___ ___ ___   ___ ___ ___ ___
 7   1   6   4   3   7   5   4   10   2   9   8

Why are there more deaths from a tornado when it occurs where a tornado rarely happens?

Floaters and Sinkers

Only one kind of rock floats, and it is an igneous rock!

All igneous rocks form from magma that hardens. So why does only one type of igneous rock float? It has to do with the way magma at the earth's surface, or lava, cools and hardens. Lava that forms basalt, a type of igneous rock, may flow a long distance before it hardens. But none of the different kinds of basalt rock float. Obsidian is an igneous rock that forms when lava cools quickly. It is smooth like glass, but it doesn't float either. Pumice, another igneous rock, has tiny holes that make the rock very light. The holes form when gases escape from the cooling lava. Some people think the holes in pumice look like the holes in a sponge. Since a sponge is light and it floats, this description makes it easy to remember which rock floats. It's pumice, the rock with tiny spongelike holes!

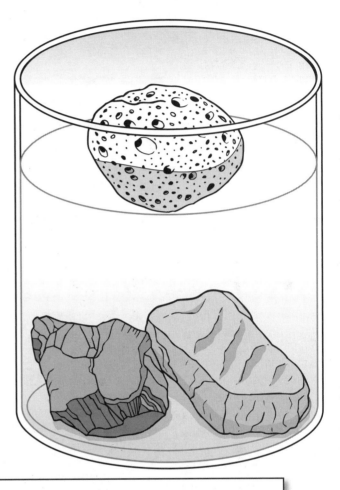

Write "T" or "F" to tell whether each sentence is true or false.

_____ 1. All igneous rocks are formed from slow-cooling lava.

_____ 2. Many kinds of igneous rocks float.

_____ 3. Pumice looks a lot like a sponge.

_____ 4. Lava that forms basalt rock hardens as soon as it reaches the earth's surface.

_____ 5. Obsidian is an igneous rock with tiny air holes.

_____ 6. Holes form in an igneous rock when gases cannot escape from the lava.

Floaters and Sinkers

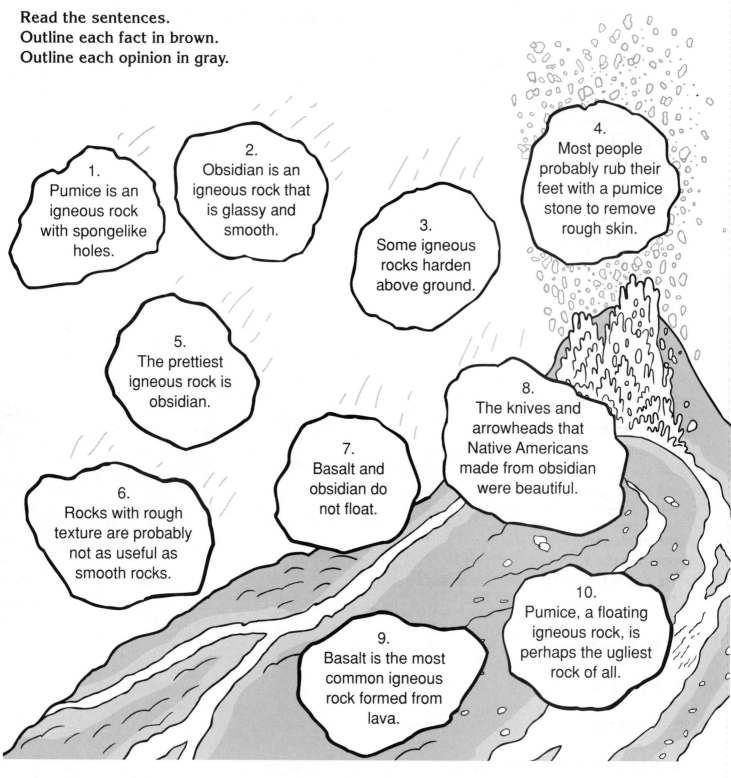

Read the sentences.
Outline each fact in brown.
Outline each opinion in gray.

1. Pumice is an igneous rock with spongelike holes.

2. Obsidian is an igneous rock that is glassy and smooth.

3. Some igneous rocks harden above ground.

4. Most people probably rub their feet with a pumice stone to remove rough skin.

5. The prettiest igneous rock is obsidian.

6. Rocks with rough texture are probably not as useful as smooth rocks.

7. Basalt and obsidian do not float.

8. The knives and arrowheads that Native Americans made from obsidian were beautiful.

9. Basalt is the most common igneous rock formed from lava.

10. Pumice, a floating igneous rock, is perhaps the ugliest rock of all.

Bonus

Pumice is very useful around a home, both in powdered form and as a stone. What do you think it might be useful for doing? Explain.

Lots of Layers

Some layers of sedimentary rocks are more than 6,000 feet deep!

Colorful layers of sedimentary rock are easy to find in the Grand Canyon. Some of the layers there are more than 6,000 feet deep. This is more than four times taller than the Empire State Building! Sedimentary rocks form very slowly. The layers in these rocks take thousands of years to form. Grains of sand and bits of clay settle on the bottoms of oceans and lakes or in river valleys. The sediment piles up layer by layer. The weight of the top layers squeezes the lower layers together. The type of sedimentary rock formed depends on the minerals that are being pressed together. You might be surprised by what you can find in sedimentary rocks. Dead plants and animals get trapped in layers of sediment. Their remains can turn into fossils over time. Imagine finding a dinosaur fossil in a rock!

Word Bank		
top	type	bottom
sediment	thousands	

Make each sentence a true fact.
Cross out the word that does not belong.
Write a word from the word bank above it.

1. Sedimentary rocks take hundreds of years to form.

2. Fossils form over time when dead plants and animals get covered by layers of lava.

3. The weight of the lower layers of sediment presses the bottom layers together.

4. Sedimentary rocks can form at the top of river valleys.

5. The size of sedimentary rock that is formed depends on the minerals that are pressed together.

Lots of Layers

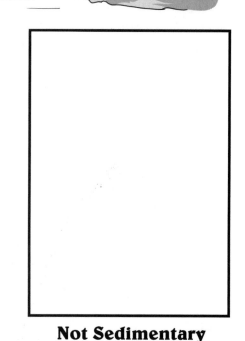

Cut out the boxes below.

Decide whether the clue on each one describes a
   sedimentary rock or another kind of rock.

Then glue each box inside the correct space.

Sedimentary   **Not Sedimentary**

 **Bonus** Conglomerate is a sedimentary rock formed when a mineral cement holds
sand and gravel together. Would a cookie with chocolate chips and nuts
make a good model of this rock? Why or why not?

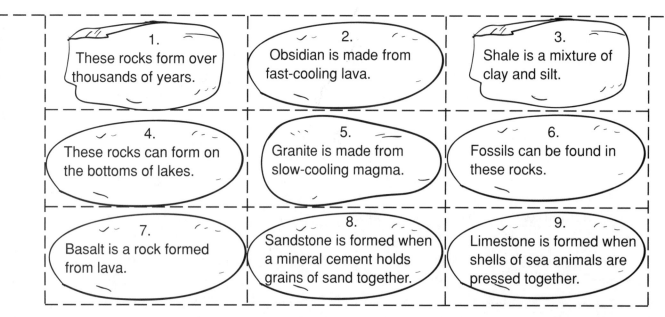

1. These rocks form over thousands of years.

2. Obsidian is made from fast-cooling lava.

3. Shale is a mixture of clay and silt.

4. These rocks can form on the bottoms of lakes.

5. Granite is made from slow-cooling magma.

6. Fossils can be found in these rocks.

7. Basalt is a rock formed from lava.

8. Sandstone is formed when a mineral cement holds grains of sand together.

9. Limestone is formed when shells of sea animals are pressed together.

Marvelous Makeovers

Metamorphic rocks are recycled rocks.

Did you know that every metamorphic rock used to be a different kind of rock? Heat and pressure change sedimentary and igneous rocks into new rocks. A metamorphic rock can also be turned into a different metamorphic rock. Heat and pressure change sedimentary rocks like shale into slate. With heat and pressure, slate becomes phyllite. Phyllite can become schist. Schist can then be turned into gneiss. When a sedimentary rock like limestone has been heated and pressed together long enough, it becomes marble. Marble is easy to carve. That's why it is a popular stone for making statues. Nature is such an amazing recycler!

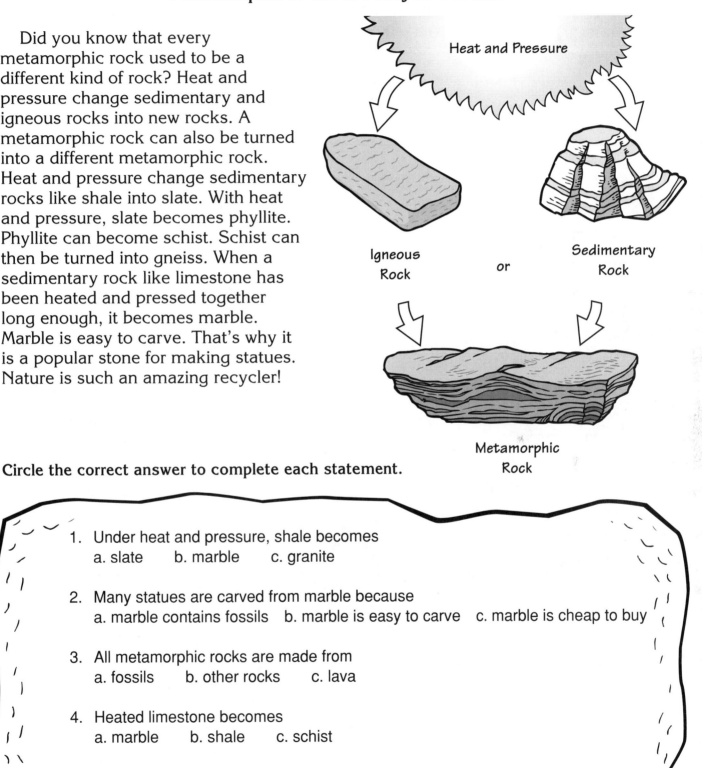

Igneous Rock   or   Sedimentary Rock

Metamorphic Rock

Circle the correct answer to complete each statement.

1. Under heat and pressure, shale becomes
   a. slate   b. marble   c. granite

2. Many statues are carved from marble because
   a. marble contains fossils   b. marble is easy to carve   c. marble is cheap to buy

3. All metamorphic rocks are made from
   a. fossils   b. other rocks   c. lava

4. Heated limestone becomes
   a. marble   b. shale   c. schist

5. Schist used to be
   a. gneiss   b. slate   c. limestone

Name _____

Marvelous Makeovers

Write a word from the word bank to complete each sentence.

1. Many famous artists have carved statues from ☐ __ __ __ __ __, which used to be the sedimentary rock limestone.

2. __ __ __ __ __ ☐ __ __ used to be the metamorphic rock slate.

3. Metamorphic rocks can be called __ __ __ __ ☐ __ __ __ rocks because they are made from other kinds of rocks.

4. Metamorphic rocks form when ☐ __ __ __ and/or __ __ ☐ __ __ __ __ __ change a rock into a different kind of rock.

5. If shale is heated and squeezed, the new rock is called __ ☐ ☐ __ __.

6. Metamorphic rocks used to be __ __ ☐ __ __ __ __, __ __ __ __ __ __ __ __ __ __ __ __, or other metamorphic rocks.

7. When the metamorphic rock schist is heated and squeezed, it forms ☐ __ ☐ __ __ __.

8. Marble is formed when ☐ __ __ __ __ __ ☐ __ __ is heated and pressed together.

WORD BANK

recycled	limestone
slate	pressure
marble	gneiss
phyllite	igneous
sedimentary	heat

Now write the boxed letters for each sentence in order in the blanks below. If your answers are correct, you'll spell the name of a famous artist who carved marble statues.

__ __ __ __ __ __ __ __ __ __ __ __
1 2 3 4 4 5 5 6 7 7 8 8

Bonus

Marble is strong and does not burn easily. Why do you think this is the reason it is used for columns, floors, and other parts of buildings?

Scratch or Be Scratched!

Nothing can scratch a diamond except another diamond.

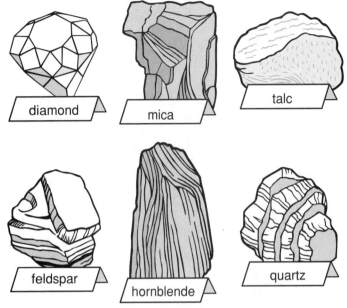

Diamonds are the hardest minerals of all. In fact, diamonds are used to make drill bits. But not all minerals are this hard. The softest mineral is talc. It can be scratched with a fingernail. So what are minerals? They are solid materials found in nature. Minerals form crystals that are the building blocks of rocks. All rocks are made of one or more minerals. Some minerals are harder than others. Some are shiny. Others are dull. Minerals are also different colors. The specks of color in a rock tell us the different minerals that make up the rock. Granite is made of the minerals feldspar, hornblende, quartz, and mica. Limestone is made mostly of calcite. The next time you pick up a rock, see if it has different colors. Then scratch it with your fingernail or another rock!

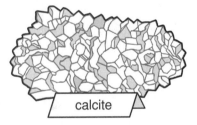

Write a word from the word bank to complete each sentence. One word will not be used.

1. Granite is made of four minerals: mica, _____, hornblende, and feldspar.

2. Minerals have _____.

3. Every rock is made of one or more _____.

4. The hardest minerals are _____.

5. The softest mineral, _____, can be easily scratched with a fingernail.

6. The rock that is made mostly of calcite is _____.

Word Bank
quartz
limestone
talc
granite
crystals
minerals
diamonds

Scratch or Be Scratched!

Use the clues on the rocks to fill in the chart.
Then answer the questions.

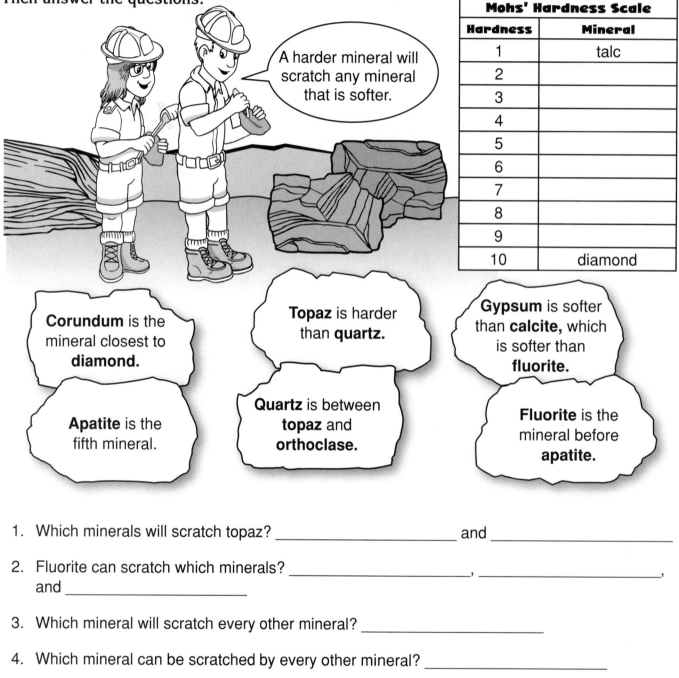

Mohs' Hardness Scale	
Hardness	**Mineral**
1	talc
2	
3	
4	
5	
6	
7	
8	
9	
10	diamond

A harder mineral will scratch any mineral that is softer.

Corundum is the mineral closest to **diamond.**

Apatite is the fifth mineral.

Topaz is harder than **quartz.**

Quartz is between **topaz** and **orthoclase.**

Gypsum is softer than **calcite,** which is softer than **fluorite.**

Fluorite is the mineral before **apatite.**

1. Which minerals will scratch topaz? _____ and _____

2. Fluorite can scratch which minerals? _____, _____,
   and _____

3. Which mineral will scratch every other mineral? _____

4. Which mineral can be scratched by every other mineral? _____

5. Which of the following minerals will not scratch quartz: topaz, calcite, or corundum?
   _____

 **Bonus** There are about 100 common minerals. The Mohs' hardness scale includes only ten minerals. How do you think scientists find out how hard or soft the other 90 minerals are?

Earth's Shifting Skin

The ground under our feet is always moving.

The earth's surface does not seem to move. But it does. That is because of its structure. The thin top layer we walk on is called the crust. If the earth were a soccer ball, its rocky skin would be about as thin as a postage stamp. The crust is made of huge curved plates that move very slowly on a thin layer of syrupy rock. The higher parts of the plates form the continents. The lower parts form the ocean floors. Rocks at the bottom of the crust are red hot. This is because the rock layers below it are thicker, hotter, and under more pressure. These factors make the solid plates shift and slide. So whether we feel it or not, the ground does move!

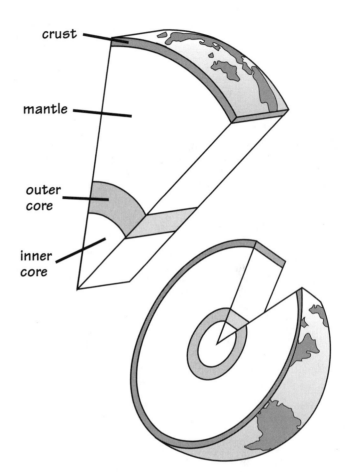

crust

mantle

outer core

inner core

Make each sentence true.
Cross out the word that does not belong.
Write a word from the word bank above it.

Word Bank

curved

thin

hot

bottom

top

mantle

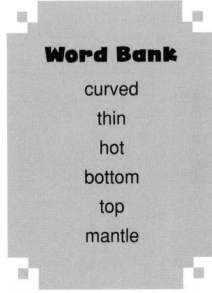

1. The bottom layer of the earth is called the crust.

2. The crust is divided into flat plates.

3. There is a layer of cold syrupy rock under the crust.

4. The layer under the crust is called the plate.

5. The earth's crust is thick and hard.

6. The rocks on the top of the crust are hot.

Earth's Shifting Skin

Use the words from the word bank to complete the puzzle.

Word Bank
continents
crust
floor
mantle
plate
slides
slowly
three

Across
2 the layer of the earth we walk on
3 one way a plate moves
7 what the higher parts of a plate form
8 a huge curved section of the earth's crust

Down
1 the part of the crust under the ocean
4 how the earth's plates move
5 the number of layers in the earth
6 the middle layer of the earth

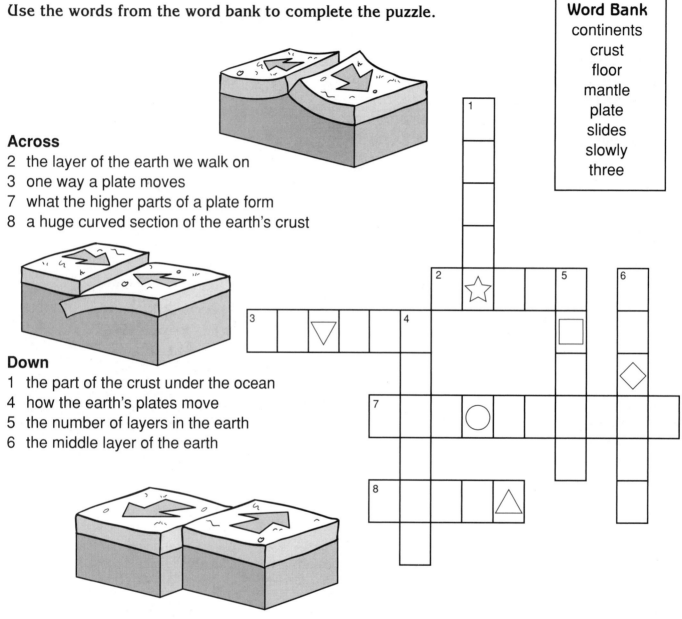

To complete the sentence below, write the letters inside the symbols above on the lines with the matching symbols.

The crust under the oceans is _ _ _ _ _ _ _ than the crust under the continents.
○ □ ▽ ◇ ◇ △ ☆

Bonus The earth's crust is its outermost layer. What other things have a crust?

  ©The Mailbox® • *Fascinating Facts: Science* • TEC61066 • Key p. 125

Name _____

A Whole Lot of Shaking Going On

Several million earthquakes occur in the world every year.

The ground shakes. Buildings fall. The ground cracks. These things can happen during an earthquake. An earthquake occurs when there is a sudden movement of the earth's plates. Earthquakes can happen anywhere in the world, but most happen along two earthquake belts where the earth's crust seems weak. A crack or break in the earth's crust along which rocks can move is called a fault. Most faults occur at the edges of plates. These plates bump, rub, or slide past each other causing pressure. If the pressure is great enough, a break in the rocks occurs. The break forces a sudden movement, sending out strong vibrations that shake the ground. Most earthquakes are small, but a large earthquake can cause a lot of damage. It can knock down houses. It can also break roads and make a crack in the ground. To know how strong an earthquake is, you can use the Richter scale!

Write a word from the word bank to complete each sentence.

1. Earthquakes happen because of the sudden _____ of the earth's plates.

2. Moving plates cause _____ to build on the rocks along the faults.

3. When a plate shifts suddenly, it causes strong _____.

4. A fault is a crack or break in the earth's _____.

5. Most faults occur at the edges of the earth's _____.

WORD BANK
pressure
plates
crust
vibrations
movement

A Whole Lot of Shaking Going On

Circle the correct word to show whether each statement is a fact or an opinion.

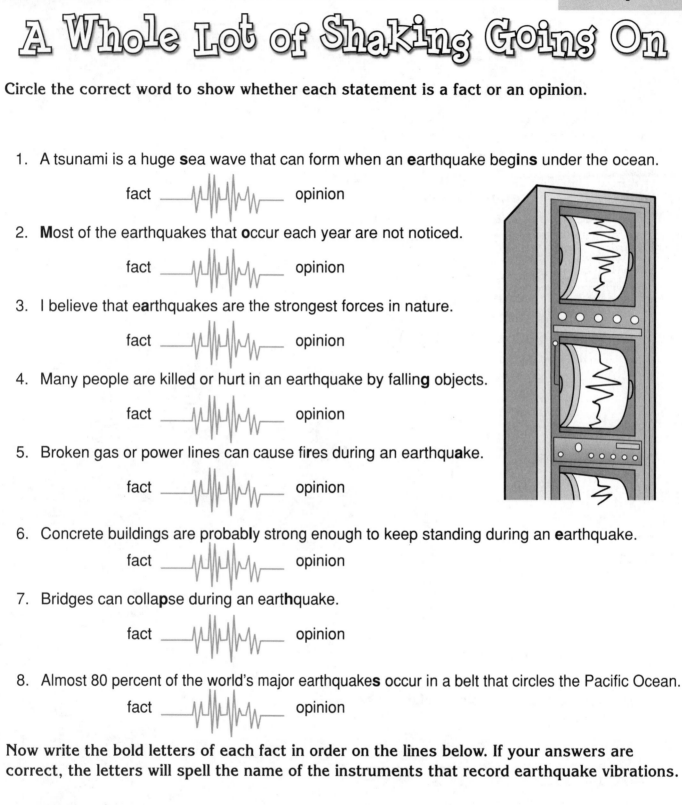

1. A tsunami is a huge **s**ea wave that can form when an **e**arthquake beg**in**s under the ocean.

    fact ———————— opinion

2. **M**ost of the earthquakes that **o**ccur each year are not noticed.

    fact ———————— opinion

3. I believe that **e**arthquakes are the strongest forces in nature.

    fact ———————— opinion

4. Many people are killed or hurt in an earthquake by fallin**g** objects.

    fact ———————— opinion

5. Broken gas or power lines can cause fi**r**es during an earthqu**a**ke.

    fact ———————— opinion

6. Concrete buildings are proba**b**ly strong enough to keep standing during an **e**arthquake.

    fact ———————— opinion

7. Bridges can colla**p**se during an eart**h**quake.

    fact ———————— opinion

8. Almost 80 percent of the world's major earthquake**s** occur in a belt that circles the Pacific Ocean.

    fact ———————— opinion

Now write the bold letters of each fact in order on the lines below. If your answers are correct, the letters will spell the name of the instruments that record earthquake vibrations.

___ ___ ___ ___ ___ ___ ___ ___ ___ ___ ___ ___ ___

Why do you think a city with more people suffers greater damage from an earthquake than a city with fewer people?

Earth's Chimneys

The area that circles the Pacific Ocean is known as the Ring of Fire because so many volcanoes erupt there.

Most volcanoes occur where the earth's large plates meet. One of those places circles the Pacific Ocean. Below these plates, the earth is hot enough to melt rocks. Melted rocks contain gases. Gases make melted rock, or magma, rise. As magma rises, it melts more rock and forms a chamber. Pressure in the chamber makes magma form a path up to the earth's surface through a crack in a weak part of the rock. Red-hot melted rock and gas then spew out of an opening, or vent, to form a mountain called a volcano. Once magma reaches the surface, it is called lava. Lava can destroy everything in its path. When lava stops flowing, a crater shaped like a bowl forms at the top of the volcano. Volcanoes can erupt again or decide to sleep for a while. Some become extinct and never erupt again!

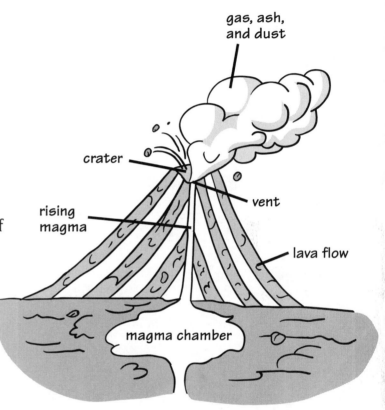

Number the events to show the order in which a volcano forms.

_____   A crater forms.

_____   Lava burns trees and buildings.

_____   Hot gases build up inside the earth.

_____   A rocky tube forms, leading to the surface.

_____   Magma and hot gases erupt through a vent.

Earth's Chimneys

Read the clues.
Then glue each label from below under the correct diagram.

CINDER CONE VOLCANO

- forms when blueberry-size pieces of hardened lava erupt and then pile up around a vent
- has a cone shape
- is small in size
- has a steep slope

1.

COMPOSITE VOLCANO

- is a medium-size mountain
- has alternate layers of lava and cinders
- has a steep peak
- has gently sloping sides
- forms from one vent
- can appear to have a perfect cone shape

2.

SHIELD VOLCANO

- is a low, wide, dome-shaped mountain
- has a gentle slope
- forms when lava spreads out in a wide area from many vents
- can be made of thousands of layers of lava that build up over time
- has many craters at the top

3.

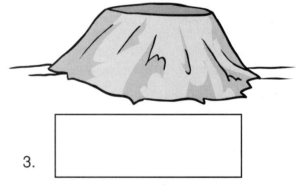

 **Bonus** Many fruits, vegetables, and other plants grow well in soil that surrounds a volcano. Why do you think this is so?

| shield volcano | cinder cone volcano | composite volcano |

Name_____

PUSHED UP AND WORN DOWN

The world's 20 highest mountains are all about five miles high.

Mountains are formed in different ways. They form when forces inside the earth act on great masses of rock. Two rocky layers can be pushed against each other until they fold or until one is pushed up higher than the other. They can also be molded into a dome. Some are made from volcanic materials.

Mountains are tall and strong, but they do not stay this way. They wear down over time because of erosion. Many things cause mountains to erode. Wind blows on a mountain and wears away soil and bits of rock. Water also plays a part. Rain can wash away soil and bits of rock. Ice can erode a mountain too. Young mountains are high and have sharp peaks. Older mountains are low and have rounded peaks. Whether mountains are young or old, they all wear down over time.

Circle the answer that completes each sentence correctly.

1. Some mountains are formed when two _____ push against each other.
   a. rocky layers   b. peaks   c. domes

2. Mountains can be folded, shaped into a dome, or made from material that erupts from _____.
   a. earthquakes   b. volcanoes   c. rivers

3. Over time, mountains _____.
   a. stay the same   b. get sharper peaks   c. erode

4. A process called _____ wears away mountains.
   a. gravity   b. erosion   c. radiation

5. Wind, water, and _____ can wear away mountains.
   a. ice   b. volcanic rock   c. folding

6. Low, rounded mountains are _____ high mountains with sharp peaks.
   a. the same age as   b. younger than   c. older than

Name _____

70

PUSHED UP AND WORN DOWN

Write each clue under the correct heading.
Then cross it off the list. The first one has been done for you.

Clues

- ~~rain~~
- valley glaciers
- dunes being moved from place to place
- continental glaciers
- rivers and streams running over the earth's surface
- air that blows and carries away loose bits of rock and soil
- groundwater that causes limestone to dissolve
- ocean waves that crash against rocks and shorelines
- air taking away sand from a desert floor

Water
- rain
- _____
- _____
- _____

Wind
- _____
- _____

Ice
- _____
- _____

Bonus Which of nature's erosion methods do you think wears down a mountain or plateau faster: wind, water, or ice? Why?

©The Mailbox® • *Fascinating Facts: Science* • TEC61066 • Key p. 126

A Puzzling Number of Planets

Pluto used to be the ninth planet.

Did you know that Earth was once thought to be the center of the solar system? People believed that the sun, the moon, and the other planets moved around Earth. Then new findings were made. People learned that Earth moves around the sun. Including Earth, there are eight planets that orbit the sun. Scientists used to say there were nine planets. But in 2006, scientists voted to change the definition of a planet. This new definition has three rules for being a planet. Pluto, which was the ninth planet, is not a planet because of the third rule. This rule says that a planet cannot have other objects in its region of orbit. Pluto has other objects in its orbit. Therefore, Pluto is no longer one of the planets. It is now called a dwarf planet. Not all scientists agree with this decision. Do you?

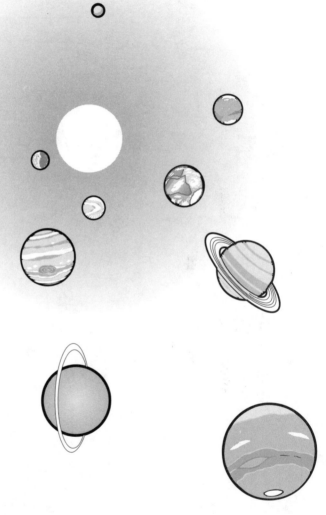

Write "true" or "false" on the line next to each sentence.

_____ 1. The sun is not a planet.

_____ 2. Some people think that Neptune should not be a planet.

_____ 3. All scientists believe Pluto is a planet.

_____ 4. Earth is the center of our solar system.

_____ 5. Experts do not agree on the number of planets.

A Puzzling Number of Planets

Find the fact that matches each planet.
Then write the number of the fact on the matching puzzle piece.

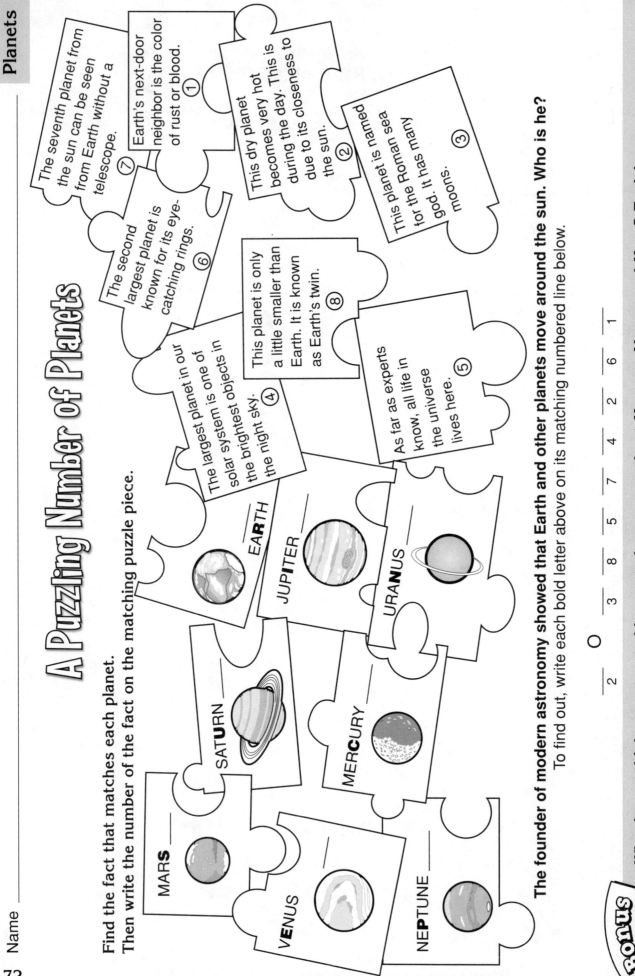

The seventh planet from the sun can be seen from Earth without a telescope. ⑦

Earth's next-door neighbor is the color of rust or blood. ①

This dry planet becomes very hot during the day. This is due to its closeness to the sun. ②

This planet is named for the Roman sea god. It has many moons. ③

The second largest planet is known for its eye-catching rings. ⑥

This planet is only a little smaller than Earth. It is known as Earth's twin. ⑧

The largest planet in our solar system is one of the brightest objects in the night sky. ④

As far as experts know, all life in the universe lives here. ⑤

MARS ___

SATURN ___

VENUS ___

EARTH ___

JUPITER ___

URANUS ___

MERCURY ___

NEPTUNE ___

The founder of modern astronomy showed that Earth and other planets move around the sun. Who is he?
To find out, write each bold letter above on its matching numbered line below.

O __ __ __ __ __ __ __ __ __ __
   2   3 8 5 7 4 2 6 1

©The Mailbox® • *Fascinating Facts: Science* • TEC61066 • Key p. 126

Bonus

Why do you think experts would want to learn more about Mercury, Venus, and Mars? Explain.

HOME, SWEET HOME

Earth is the only planet in the solar system that can support life.

Would you like to live on another planet? Could it be done? The two planets closest to the sun are too hot. The planets beyond Earth are too cold. But Earth is just the right distance from the sun. It gets the right amount of heat. Earth provides the oxygen and water that people, plants, and animals need to survive. Earth is also protected by special layers of air called the atmosphere. The atmosphere covers Earth and keeps it from freezing. It also filters the sun's strong rays and provides rain. These factors make Earth the best place for all living things. It's easy to see why no other planet measures up!

Circle the best answer.

1. What is the main idea of the paragraph?
   a. Earth is the third planet from the sun.
   b. Earth is the only planet in our solar system that can meet the needs of living things.
   c. Earth gets heat from the sun.

2. What keeps Earth from getting too hot or too cold?
   a. the sun's rays
   b. the rain
   c. its atmosphere

3. How does the atmosphere help provide water for Earth?
   a. Clouds in the atmosphere bring rain.
   b. It covers only part of Earth.
   c. It blocks sunlight.

4. This passage could also be called _____.
   a. "Mars is Too Cold"
   b. "No Planet Compares to Earth"
   c. "The Best is Yet to Come"

Name _____

HOME, SWEET HOME

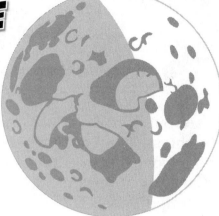

Complete each sentence with a word from the word bank.

Thermosphere

1. The space __ __ __ __ __ __ __ cruises here high above Earth.

2. The aurora borealis, or northern __ __ __ __ __ __, can also be seen on Earth at night in the far north. Most auroras are green, but some may be red or purple.

Mesosphere

3. Strong __ __ __ __ __ blow in this layer.

4. __ __ __ __ __ __ __ trails look like shooting stars.

Stratosphere

5. The __ __ __ __ __ layer in this part of the atmosphere absorbs the sun's harmful rays.

6. __ __ __ __ __ __ __ __ __ __ can fly here above the weather.

Troposphere

7. This layer is where almost all __ __ __ __ __ __ __, whether pleasant or severe, occurs.

8. The __ __ __ __ __ __ __ __ __ __ effect traps the sun's heat here to warm Earth's surface.

Word Bank

airplanes	shuttle	ozone
greenhouse	winds	lights
weather		meteor

What do you think would happen if one of these layers disappeared? Explain.

Name _____

Our Bright Night-Light

The moon is dark red during a lunar eclipse.

About 238,857 miles from Earth is the brightest object in the night sky. This close neighbor is our moon. The moon does not shine. It just reflects light from the sun. Amazing things happen as this large ball of rocky material makes its monthly trip around Earth. As the moon orbits Earth, the amount of sunlight the moon reflects back to Earth changes. This causes the moon to look as though it's changing shape. These changes are called phases. Another amazing thing is an eclipse. There are two types. A solar eclipse occurs when a new moon passes between Earth and the sun. This causes the moon's shadow to move across Earth. A lunar eclipse occurs when a full moon moves through Earth's shadow. This makes the moon appear red. Why? It's because Earth's atmosphere bends red rays from the sun!

Answer the questions.

1. Why does the moon have phases? _____

    _____

2. About how long does it take the moon to make one trip around Earth? _____

3. During a lunar eclipse, where is the moon? _____

    _____

4. What keeps sunlight from shining on the moon during a lunar eclipse? _____

    _____

5. From where does the moon receive the light that it reflects? _____

    _____

Our Bright Night-Light

Complete each sentence with a word from the word bank.
Use the diagram for help.

Sun

Lunar Eclipse

Earth

Moon

In a lunar eclipse,

_____

blocks sunlight from the

_____ . The

_____ is in

complete darkness and has a

_____ glow.

Sun

Solar Eclipse

Moon

Earth

In a solar eclipse, the

_____

blocks sunlight from

_____ . The

_____ casts

a _____ on

Earth.

Word Bank

Earth	Earth	moon	moon
moon	moon	red	shadow

Bonus   A lunar eclipse lasts longer than a solar eclipse. Why do you think this is so?

©The Mailbox® • *Fascinating Facts: Science* • TEC61066 • Key p. 126

Name _____

Goodness, Gracious, Great Balls of Gas!

Even without a telescope, you can see about 3,000 stars on a clear night.

Do you like to gaze at stars? Stars are large balls of hot gases that produce their own light. There are many trillions of stars. Stars can be seen because the intense heat they give off makes them glow. Some stars are brighter than others. They come in many sizes and are different colors. Some stars are hundreds of times bigger than the sun. Some are the size of Earth, and others are smaller. Blue stars are hotter than our own yellow star, the sun. Red stars are cooler. Ancient astronomers grouped stars to make them easier to study. These star groups are called constellations. They are named for objects, animals, gods, and heroes. Which constellation is easiest for you to pick out?

Write a word or phrase from the paragraph above to complete each sentence.

1. About _____ stars can be seen without a telescope on a clear night.

2. Stars are large balls of hot _____.

3. Stars shine because _____ causes them to glow.

4. _____ stars are cooler than the sun.

5. Some stars are bigger than the _____.

78 Name _____

Goodness, Gracious, Great Balls of Gas!

Create two constellations by coloring a star to plot each ordered pair of numbers. Connect the stars as you go.

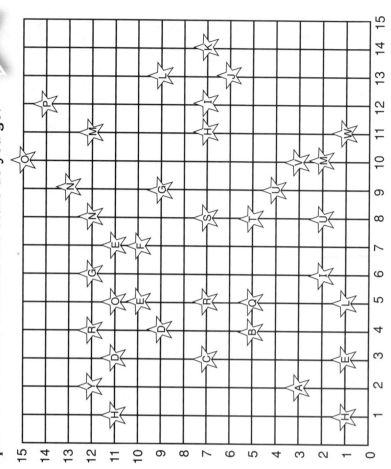

**Draco
(the dragon)**

(2, 3)
(4, 5)
(3, 7)
(4, 9)
(5, 10)
(7, 10)
(9, 9)
(11, 7)
(12, 7)
(13, 6)
(14, 7)
(13, 9)
(11, 12)
(9, 13)
(10, 15)
(12, 14)
(11, 12)

**Ursa Minor
(the Little Dipper)**

(8, 5)
(5, 5)
(5, 7)
(8, 7)
(8, 5)
(9, 4)
(10, 3)
(11, 1)

Stars are mainly made of two gases.
Write the letters of the uncolored stars
in the top half of the grid and then those
in the bottom half of the grid from left to
right to spell their names:

_____ and _____.

Bonus

Why do you think the position of a constellation seems to move in
the sky from one night to the next?

Space Snowballs

Comets cannot be seen without a telescope until they get close to the sun.

Imagine a snowball ten miles wide. That's the size of some comets. Comets are made of ice and dust. When a comet's orbit brings it near the sun, its icy surface melts. The bits of ice and dust that fly away from a comet's body form a stream behind it. Dust in the ice reflects sunlight. This is one reason a comet can be seen. As a comet moves away from the sun, its gases freeze again. Then its tail disappears, and the comet can no longer be seen. In time, a comet will return if it is not melted by the sun or it does not crash into a planet or a moon. Halley's comet is famous. But you may be able to see it just once in your lifetime. Why? It only crosses Earth's orbit about once every 76 years!

Write "Yes" or "No" to answer each question. Then give a reason for your answer.

1. Could someone without a telescope see a comet if it were near the planet Saturn? _____

   _____

2. Halley's comet was last seen in 1986. Is it likely that you may see it when it returns? _____

   _____

3. Do comets ever die? _____

   _____

4. Could a comet be ten miles wide? _____

   _____

Name _____

Space Snowballs

Glue each box to the part of the diagram that it describes. Two have been done for you.

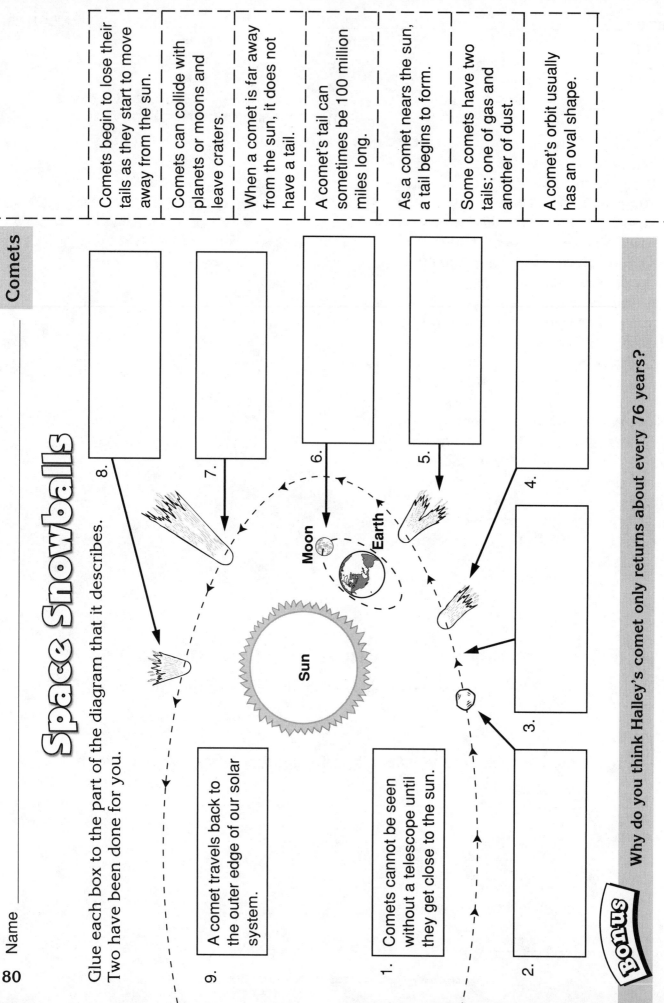

8.

7.

6.

5.

4.

3.

9. A comet travels back to the outer edge of our solar system.

1. Comets cannot be seen without a telescope until they get close to the sun.

2.

Sun

Moon

Earth

Comets begin to lose their tails as they start to move away from the sun.

Comets can collide with planets or moons and leave craters.

When a comet is far away from the sun, it does not have a tail.

A comet's tail can sometimes be 100 million miles long.

As a comet nears the sun, a tail begins to form.

Some comets have two tails: one of gas and another of dust.

A comet's orbit usually has an oval shape.

Bonus Why do you think Halley's comet only returns about every 76 years?

Tiny Planets

Many scientists think of asteroids as minor, or small, planets.

Do you know anything about Ceres? It is just one of the named asteroids in our solar system. Some scientists call asteroids minor planets because they orbit the sun just as planets do. In fact, some asteroids even have their own moons! Asteroids can be made of rock or metal. And, just like planets, they come in all sizes. The biggest asteroids are hundreds of miles wide. The smallest ones may be just a few feet wide or even smaller. Some asteroids are found far out in space. But most of them are closer to Earth, between Mars and Jupiter in an area called the Main Belt. Asteroids are known to crash into things. Fortunately, our atmosphere causes most of these minor planets to burn up before they reach Earth's surface!

Circle the correct answer.

1. What is the main idea of the paragraph?
   a. Earth will not be hit by an asteroid.
   b. Asteroids have a lot in common with planets.
   c. Asteroids orbit the sun like planets do.
   d. Asteroids can be found in space.

2. Asteroids can be made of
   _____.
   a. rock or metal
   b. dust or rock
   c. ice and metal
   d. dust and metal

3. The paragraph could also be titled
   _____.
   a. Heavy-Metal Asteroids
   b. Minor Planets With Moons
   c. They Are Not Dangerous
   d. Weird Rocks

4. Most asteroids can be found between _____.
   a. Mars and Saturn
   b. Jupiter and Neptune
   c. Mars and Jupiter
   d. Jupiter and Saturn

Tiny Planets

Cut out each event card.
Read the clue.
Then glue the card to the timeline.

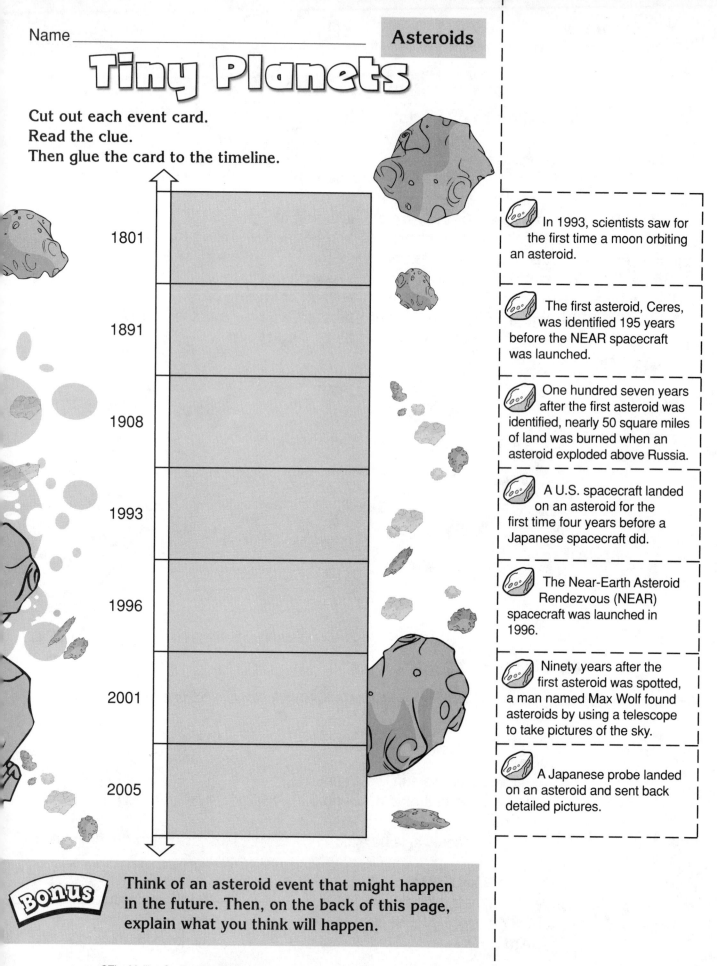

1801

1891

1908

1993

1996

2001

2005

In 1993, scientists saw for the first time a moon orbiting an asteroid.

The first asteroid, Ceres, was identified 195 years before the NEAR spacecraft was launched.

One hundred seven years after the first asteroid was identified, nearly 50 square miles of land was burned when an asteroid exploded above Russia.

A U.S. spacecraft landed on an asteroid for the first time four years before a Japanese spacecraft did.

The Near-Earth Asteroid Rendezvous (NEAR) spacecraft was launched in 1996.

Ninety years after the first asteroid was spotted, a man named Max Wolf found asteroids by using a telescope to take pictures of the sky.

A Japanese probe landed on an asteroid and sent back detailed pictures.

Bonus   Think of an asteroid event that might happen in the future. Then, on the back of this page, explain what you think will happen.

Movin' Meteors

Shooting stars are meteors moving through the sky.

Millions of meteors enter Earth's atmosphere every day. They appear in the sky as quick streaks of light, and then they are gone. They can travel as fast as 44 miles per second. That is 158,400 miles per hour! After they enter Earth's atmosphere, most meteors get very hot and burn up. The few that do not burn up and make it to Earth are called meteorites. When large meteorites hit the ground, they often leave an impact crater. The famous Meteor Crater in Arizona measures over 4,000 feet wide and 550 feet deep. Meteors are usually made from pieces of asteroids, comets, or pieces of the same material from which planets are made. Some meteors are super heavy, weighing as much as 300,000 tons!

Change one word in each sentence to make the statement true.

1. Meteors look like a slow streak of light in the sky.

2. A meteor turns into a comet once it reaches Earth.

3. Meteors can weigh as little as 300,000 tons.

4. Meteors are usually made from pieces of asteroids, comets, or pieces of the same material from which meteors are made.

5. Most meteors freeze before we can see them.

Name _____

Movin' Meteors

Crack the code at the bottom of the page. Then answer each question.

1. What do some people call meteors?

$\overline{57}\ \overline{24}\ \overline{45}\ \overline{45}\ \overline{60}\ \overline{27}\ \overline{42}\ \overline{21}$

$\overline{57}\ \overline{60}\ \overline{3}\ \overline{54}\ \overline{57}$

2. What are pieces of comets that stream through the air called?

$\overline{39}\ \overline{15}\ \overline{60}\ \overline{15}\ \overline{45}\ \overline{54}$

$\overline{57}\ \overline{24}\ \overline{45}\ \overline{69}\ \overline{15}\ \overline{54}$

3. Where have thousands of meteorites been found and studied?

$\overline{3}\ \overline{42}\ \overline{60}\ \overline{3}\ \overline{54}\ \overline{9}\ \overline{60}\ \overline{27}\ \overline{9}\ \overline{3}$

4. What are meteors usually made of other than pieces of the same material from which planets are formed?

$\overline{48}\ \overline{27}\ \overline{15}\ \overline{9}\ \overline{15}\ \overline{57}\ \overline{45}\ \overline{18}$

$\overline{3}\ \overline{57}\ \overline{60}\ \overline{15}\ \overline{54}\ \overline{45}\ \overline{27}\ \overline{12}\ \overline{57}$

$\overline{9}\ \overline{45}\ \overline{39}\ \overline{15}\ \overline{60}\ \overline{57}$

$\overline{45}\ \overline{54}$

5. How many impact craters and basins have been found on Earth?

$\overline{45}\ \overline{66}\ \overline{15}\ \overline{54}\ \overline{45}\ \overline{42}\ \overline{15}$

$\overline{24}\ \overline{63}\ \overline{42}\ \overline{12}\ \overline{54}\ \overline{15}\ \overline{12}$

$\overline{60}\ \overline{69}\ \overline{15}\ \overline{42}\ \overline{60}\ \overline{75}$

A	B	C	D	E	F	G	H	I	J	K	L	M	N	O	P	Q	R	S	T	U	V	W	X	Y	Z
3		12									36														78

BONUS

What kind of damage could a large meteorite cause if it crashed in your town? Explain.

Solid as a Rock!

A solid resists changing its shape.

Everything on the earth is made of atoms. Atoms are so small that you cannot see them. They combine to form molecules. When molecules are packed closely together and move slowly, they form a solid. Solids are strong and have a definite volume and shape. A book, a rock, and a copper pipe all are solids. Each molecule of a solid vibrates back and forth without leaving its place. This allows a solid to keep its shape. Force is required to change a solid's shape. Rubber stretches. Glass can break. But if a solid is broken, its pieces still have a definite shape and volume. Not all solids look the same. A plastic sandwich bag is clear. A gold necklace can be shiny. But however they look or are shaped, these objects still have one thing in common: each one is a solid.

Answer each question.

1. How are solids alike? _____
   _____

2. How are solids different? _____
   _____

3. What is needed for a solid to change shape? _____
   _____

4. List five solids found in the classroom. _____
   _____

Solid as a Rock!

Complete each sentence with a word from the word bank.

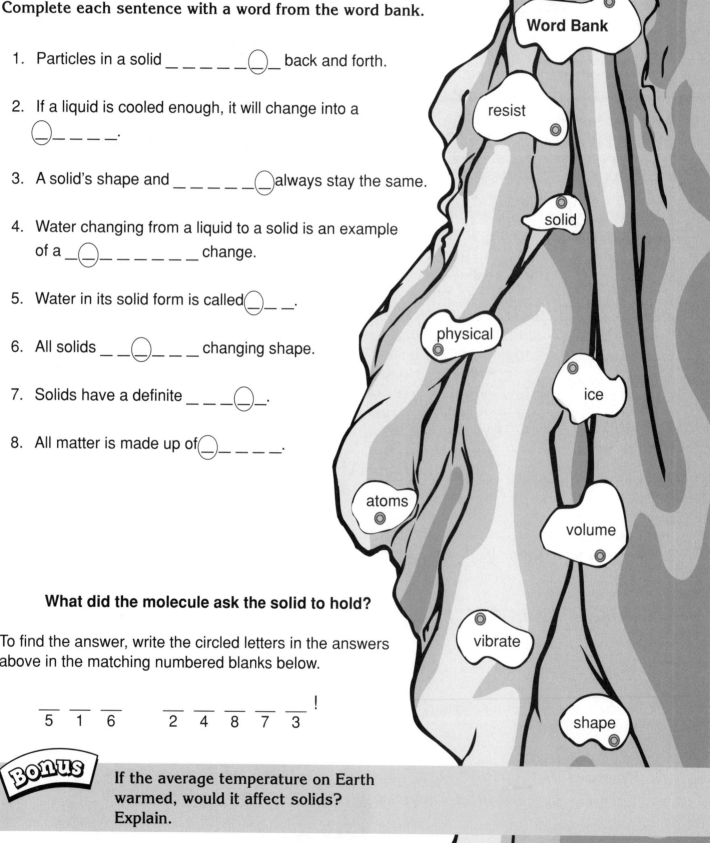

Word Bank

resist

solid

physical

ice

volume

atoms

vibrate

shape

1. Particles in a solid _ _ _ _ _○_ back and forth.

2. If a liquid is cooled enough, it will change into a
   ○_ _ _ _.

3. A solid's shape and _ _ _ _ _○ always stay the same.

4. Water changing from a liquid to a solid is an example
   of a _○_ _ _ _ _ _ change.

5. Water in its solid form is called ○_ _.

6. All solids _ _○_ _ _ changing shape.

7. Solids have a definite _ _ _○_.

8. All matter is made up of ○_ _ _ _.

What did the molecule ask the solid to hold?

To find the answer, write the circled letters in the answers
above in the matching numbered blanks below.

___ ___ ___   ___ ___ ___ ___ ___ !
 5   1   6   2   4   8   7   3

Bonus

If the average temperature on Earth
warmed, would it affect solids?
Explain.

Name _____

Nothing can live without one very important liquid—water.

What do water, oil, and honey have in common? All are liquids. A liquid is a special kind of matter. Liquids take the shape of the container they are in. Pour some water in a cup. Then pour it into a pan. The water changes shape, but it is still the same water. Liquids change shape because their molecules are not as close together as molecules in solids. Liquids usually are not as strong as solids either. A rock is hard to break. But it is easy to push your hand through water. Liquids can change forms too. If water gets very cold, it turns into a solid—ice. If water gets hot enough, it turns into a gas—steam. Liquids are amazing!

**Mark out the word that makes each sentence false.
Write a new word in the blank to make the sentence true.**

1. Liquids take the size of the container they are in. _____

2. A liquid usually is stronger than a solid. _____

3. When water changes into a solid, it is called steam. _____

4. Molecules are not packed closely together in a solid. _____

Name _____

LET IT FLOW!

Write a letter in the blank for each ordered pair. If your answers are correct, you will spell the words that complete each sentence.

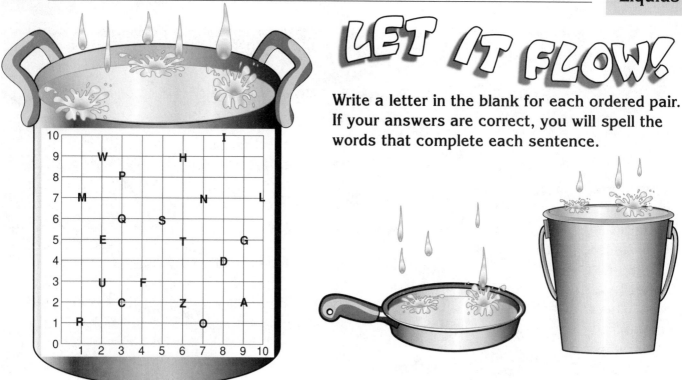

1. Liquid ___ ___ ___ ___ ___ ___ ___ ___ ___are close together but not as close as
   (3, 8) (9, 2) (1, 1) (6, 5) (8, 10) (3, 2) (10, 7) (2, 5) (5, 6)

   those in a ___ ___ ___ ___ ___. They are closer together than those in a ___ ___ ___.
   (5, 6) (7, 1) (10, 7) (8, 10) (8, 4)   (9, 5) (9, 2) (5, 6)

2. A liquid takes the ___ ___ ___ ___ ___ of the container it is in. A solid has a
   (5, 6) (6, 9) (9, 2) (3, 8) (2, 5)

   ___ ___ ___ ___ ___ ___ ___ ___   ___ ___ ___ ___ ___ of its own.
   (8, 4) (2, 5) (4, 3) (8, 10) (7, 7) (8, 10) (6, 5) (2, 5)   (5, 6) (6, 9) (9, 2) (3, 8) (2, 5)

3. Solids are usually ___ ___ ___ ___ ___ ___ ___ ___ than liquids. But a liquid is too
   (5, 6) (6, 5) (1, 1) (7, 1) (7, 7) (9, 5) (2, 5) (1, 1)

   strong to be ___ ___ ___ ___ ___ ___ ___ ___ into less space.
   (5, 6) (3, 6) (2, 3) (2, 5) (2, 5) (6, 2) (2, 5) (8, 4)

4. ___ ___ ___ ___ ___ is the most common ___ ___ ___ ___ ___ ___ on the earth.
   (2, 9) (9, 2) (6, 5) (2, 5) (1, 1)   (10, 7) (8, 10) (3, 6) (2, 3) (8, 10) (8, 4)

5. Liquids change into ___ ___ ___ ___ ___ if heated enough. Liquids change into
   (9, 5) (9, 2) (5, 6) (2, 5) (5, 6)

   ___ ___ ___ ___ ___ ___ if cooled enough.
   (5, 6) (7, 1) (10, 7) (8, 10) (8, 4) (5, 6)

Bonus

List three different liquids. Can each liquid change into a solid?
Can each liquid change into a gas? Explain.

HIGH-SPEED MOLECULES

A gas particle moves at about the speed of sound.

Magnification

Gases are one of three states of matter. They are not like solids and liquids. Most gases cannot be seen. The air we breathe is a mixture of nitrogen, oxygen, and other gases. If you take a deep breath, you cannot see air moving into your nose. But you can feel it fill your lungs. Gas particles can have different weights, but they all move quickly. They move even faster if the gas is hot. They move slower if the gas is cold. They move, collide, and bounce around in the space they are in all the time. In fact, a gas will fully fill its container. If a container is small, the particles move closer together. If a container is large, the particles spread farther apart. But when a container is opened, the gases from inside will rush outside, moving at more than 1,000 feet per second!

Use facts from the passage to complete the chart.

	Solid	Liquid	Gas
Shape	definite shape	no definite shape— takes shape of its container	
Movement of Particles	particles vibrate back and forth but stay in the same place	particles move back and forth and from place to place	
Space	always takes up the same amount of space	always takes up the same amount of space	

HIGH-SPEED MOLECULES

Decide whether each sentence is true or false.
Then color the correct molecule.

	True	False	
1.	◯	◯	Gas is the most important state of matter.
2.	◯	◯	A gas has no definite shape or volume.
3.	◯	◯	Gas particles move slowly.
4.	◯	◯	Air is made up mainly of oxygen.
5.	◯	◯	For humans, the most important gas in the air is oxygen.
6.	◯	◯	A gas can be squeezed into a smaller container.
7.	◯	◯	A gas moves more quickly when it is hot.
8.	◯	◯	All gas particles are about the same weight.

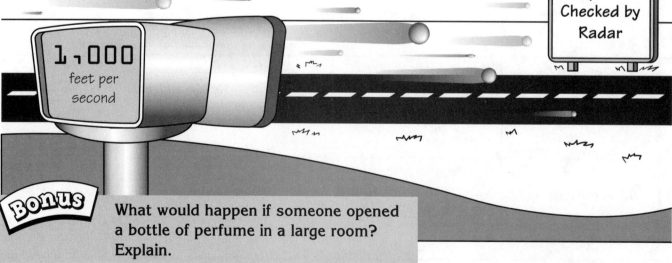

1,000 feet per second

Speed Checked by Radar

Bonus

What would happen if someone opened a bottle of perfume in a large room? Explain.

Mix It Up!

**Mixtures are all around you. Apple pie, ocean water,
and the air you breathe are just a few.**

Matter is made of molecules. Some matter, like water, is made
of one kind of molecule. Matter that is made of two or more
different substances is called a mixture. Mixing different substances
together creates a physical change. Trail mix is a mixture of many
solids. Each small raisin, peanut, pretzel, and cereal piece in it is
different from the mixture as a whole. The mix is easy to sort, and
each single piece is still distinct. Oil-and-vinegar salad
dressing is a liquid mixture. The air that we
breathe is a mixture of gases. Nitrogen
and oxygen make up the largest parts
of air. Even your own blood, sweat,
and tears are examples of mixtures!

Word Bank

oil	mixture
oxygen	liquid
physical	solid
gases	

**Complete each sentence with a word from the word bank.
Some words will not be used.**

1. A _____ is made of two or more different substances.

2. Salad dressing is an example of a _____ mixture.

3. Trail mix is a mixture in _____ form.

4. Air is a mixture of _____.

5. A mixture results in a _____ change.

Mix It Up!

Decide whether each sentence is a fact or an opinion.
If the sentence is a fact, color the piece of trail mix blue.
If the sentence is an opinion, color the piece of trail mix red.

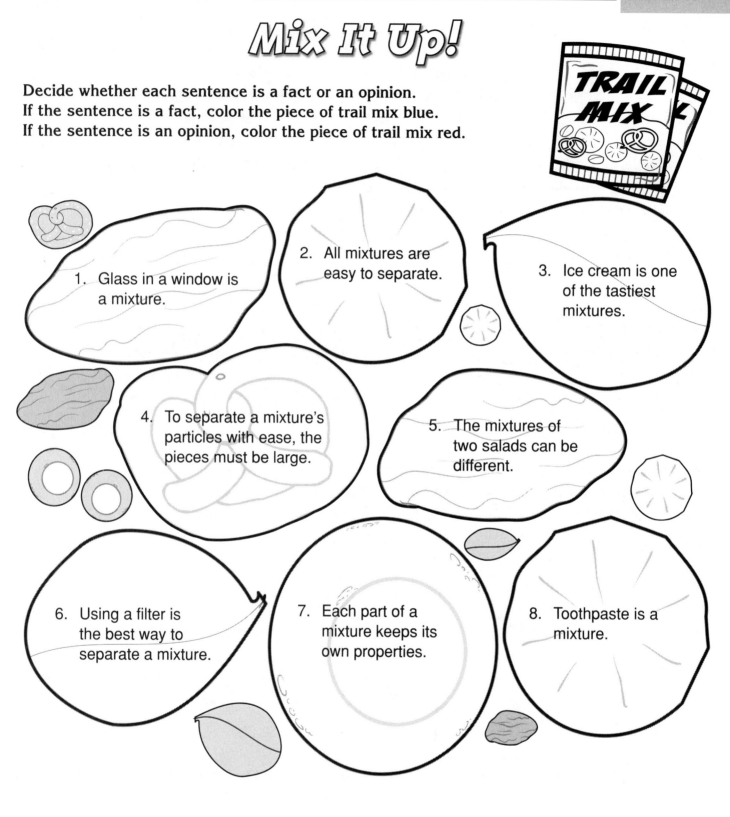

1. Glass in a window is a mixture.

2. All mixtures are easy to separate.

3. Ice cream is one of the tastiest mixtures.

4. To separate a mixture's particles with ease, the pieces must be large.

5. The mixtures of two salads can be different.

6. Using a filter is the best way to separate a mixture.

7. Each part of a mixture keeps its own properties.

8. Toothpaste is a mixture.

Bonus

List three mixtures. Explain why each one is a mixture.

Solutions Matter

Kool-Aid and gasoline are both solutions.

Dirt and water can be mixed to form a muddy mixture. Then they can be separated again when the dirt sinks to the bottom of the water. But some substances mix together and are not easy to separate. They are evenly spread throughout the mixture. Such substances are called solutions. A solution is a special kind of mixture. Sugar stirred into a cup of hot coffee forms a solution. The sugar is the smaller amount. It dissolves in the coffee and is called the solute. The coffee is the greater amount. It dissolves the sugar and is called the solvent. Once the sugar is dissolved in the coffee, it can no longer be seen. But it can be tasted. On the other hand, a solvent such as the coffee can only dissolve so much sugar. Any extra sugar remains in the bottom of the cup. Every solvent has its limits!

Match each word to its definition.

_____ 1. solvent

_____ 2. dissolve

_____ 3. solution

_____ 4. solute

_____ 5. mixture

a. a mixture in which the properties of the substances are spread evenly

b. the substance that is dissolved

c. two or more substances that keep their own properties when combined

d. disappear

e. something that dissolves another substance

Solutions Matter

Read the clues.
Unscramble the letters to spell a word in the word bank.
Then circle the answers in the puzzle.

1. All solutions are _____ (xretmuis).

2. If a gas or a solid dissolves in a liquid, it is _____ (bseullo).

3. In a solution, different particles are spread _____ (neelyv).

4. The substance in a solution that dissolves the other is the _____ (vnloset).

5. When one substance can no longer absorb any more of the other, the solution is _____ (dsruaatte).

6. In a solution, the substance that is dissolved is the _____ (ustoel).

7. Not all mixtures are _____ (ulositnso).

h	r	e	t	u	l	o	s	v	s
p	e	y	e	b	o	w	f	o	a
s	e	v	n	l	y	k	l	t	t
o	l	r	e	m	k	u	q	a	u
l	b	x	c	n	t	f	a	l	r
v	u	c	o	i	l	b	p	v	a
e	l	a	o	t	z	y	l	u	t
n	o	n	d	s	e	u	e	c	e
t	s	n	b	l	h	f	e	u	d
g	d	m	i	x	t	u	r	e	s

Word Bank

saturated   evenly

mixtures   solute

soluble   solvent

solutions

 **What effect does stirring have on substances in a solution? Explain.**

Hot Stuff!

Heat flows in only one direction.

Why does the ice in a glass of soda melt? It is because heat always travels from hotter objects to colder objects. The hotter a substance is, the faster its molecules move. Liquid molecules move more freely than solid molecules. The molecules in soda at room temperature move faster than those in an ice cube. This is because the soda is warmer. When the soda is poured into a cup of ice, some of the warmer soda molecules pass as heat into the colder molecules of the ice. The ice molecules begin to move faster, causing the ice to become warm enough to melt. Can you picture what would happen to the soda if heat did not travel one path?

Soda: 65° F

Ice: 30° F

SODA

Cross out the word that makes each sentence false.
Then write a word on the line to make the statement true.

1. Heat travels from hot objects to hotter objects.

   _____

2. The hotter a substance is, the slower its molecules move.

   _____

3. The ice in a glass of soda melts because the soda is colder.

   _____

4. Ice always travels in one direction.

   _____

5. Slow-moving molecules cause ice to melt.

   _____

Hot Stuff!

Circle the object that has more heat energy. Then draw an arrow to show the direction the heat will travel.

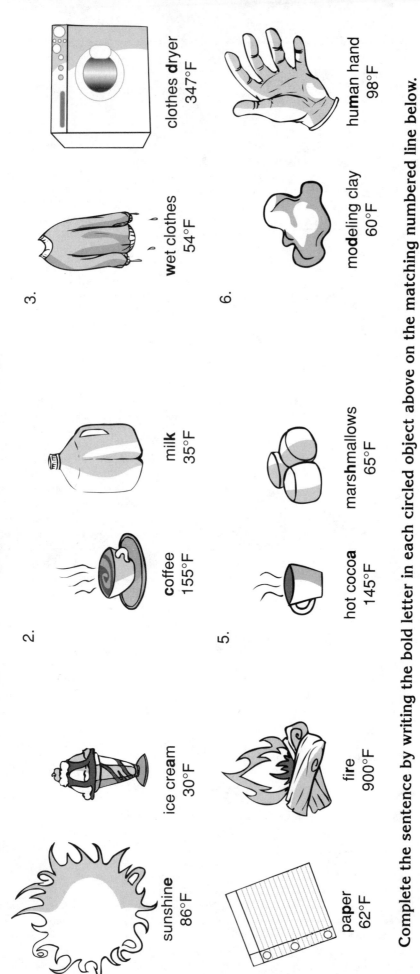

1. sunshine 86°F   ice cream 30°F

2. coffee 155°F   milk 35°F

3. wet clothes 54°F   clothes dryer 347°F

4. paper 62°F

5. hot cocoa 145°F   fire 900°F

6. marshmallows 65°F   modeling clay 60°F   human hand 98°F

Complete the sentence by writing the bold letter in each circled object above on the matching numbered line below.

Heat always moves from w
___ ___ ___ ___ ___ to ___ ___ ___ ___ ___ ___ objects.
     5   4   6   1   4   2   2   3   1   4

Bonus

Use what you know about heat to explain why ice cream is likely to melt outside on a warm day.

THE LIGHT OF LIFE

Without light, there would be no life on the earth.

Radiant energy is any energy that can freely travel from its source through space. We can only see a fraction of the different kinds of radiant energy. Light is a visible form of radiant energy. It comes from both natural and man-made sources, such as the sun and lightbulbs. Whatever the source, there would be no life on the earth without light. Humans have come to depend on light for food, heat, and even the air we breathe. Light helps plants grow, and many of the animals we rely on eat plants for food. Both humans and animals need plants to produce oxygen so we can breathe. If there were no light, we could not survive.

Circle the letter of the answer that best completes each sentence.

1. Light is a form of _____.
   a. energy
   b. space
   c. air

2. The sun is a type of _____ light.
   a. man-made
   b. natural
   c. invisible

3. _____ need light to live.
   a. plants and animals
   b. humans
   c. all of the above

4. An example of man-made light is _____.
   a. the sun
   b. the earth
   c. a lightbulb

Light

THE LIGHT OF LIFE

Cut out the boxes. Sort each fact. Then glue each box to the correct side of the chart.

Earth
With
Light

Earth
Without
Light

BONUS If the sun did not rise tomorrow, how would your life change? Explain.

©The Mailbox® • *Fascinating Facts: Science* • TEC61066 • Key p. 128

| too cold for life |
| right temperature for life |
| complete darkness |
| day and night |
| no seasons |
| fall, winter, spring, summer |
| no water cycle |
| working water cycle |
| no wind or rain |
| wind and rain |
| no food or oxygen |
| plenty of food and oxygen |

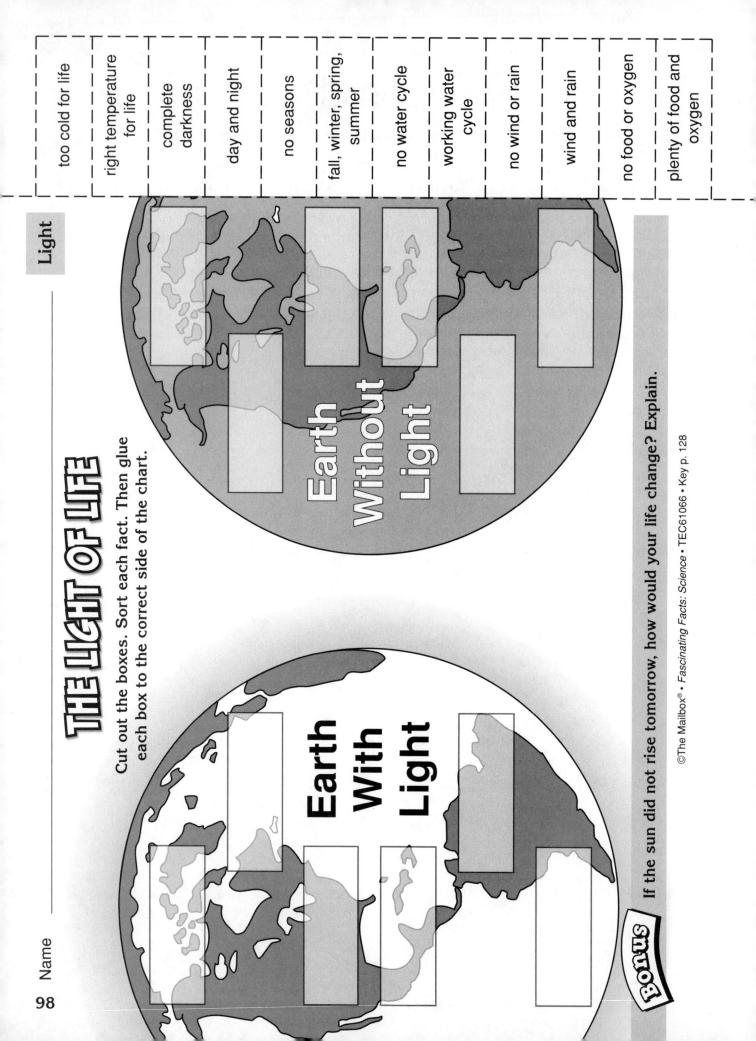

Have You Heard?

There is no sound in space.

Like dominoes, a vibrating object can set a chain of events in motion. Sound begins as the vibration of an object. When an object vibrates, it causes any substance around it to vibrate too. Those vibrations then travel in waves through the substance. When the sound waves reach our ears, the vibrations are turned into signals for the brain. But, if one link in the chain is missing, then no sound is made. So, can an astronaut floating in space hear the door to his spaceship close? No, because when the door vibrates, there is no substance in space for the sound waves to travel through. The door makes no sound.

Unscramble the word in parentheses to complete each sentence.

1. Sound travels in ___ ___ ___ ___ ___. (asvew)

2. In order to create a sound, an object must first ___ ___ ___ ___ ___ ___ ___. (birvtae)

3. Sound vibrations will travel through any ___ ___ ___ ___ ___ ___ ___ ___ ___. (ecnatsbus)

4. The ear turns sound waves into ___ ___ ___ ___ ___ ___ ___ for the brain. (nslasgi)

5. There is no ___ ___ ___ ___ ___ in space. (uodns)

Name _____

Have You Heard?

Look at the diagram below. Number the sentences from 1 to 8 to show the order in which the events occur.

☐ The sound waves reach students' ears.

☐ The ears turn the vibrations into signals for the students' brains.

☐ The bell's vibrations cause the air around it to vibrate.

☐ The students leave for home.

☐ The school bell rings at 3:15 PM.

☐ The vibrations keep moving through the air as sound waves.

☐ The sound waves travel in all directions.

☐ Their brains decide what sound the students hear.

BONUS Imagine that one of the events above is missing. How would this affect the student's ability to hear the bell ring? Explain.

©The Mailbox® • *Fascinating Facts: Science* • TEC61066 • Key p. 128

Opposites Attract

Some small animals have magnets in their bodies.

All magnets have two ends. One end is called the north pole. The other end is called the south pole. If the north and south poles of two magnets are lined up, they will push away from each other, or *repel*. If the south pole of one magnet is lined up with the north pole of another, the two magnets will pull toward each other, or *attract*. Earth is a giant magnet that has a north pole and a south pole. Some birds, insects, and fish have tiny magnets with poles inside their bodies. Scientists think that these animals use their magnets to find their way when they migrate. Maybe that's how those animals know which direction to swim, crawl, or fly!

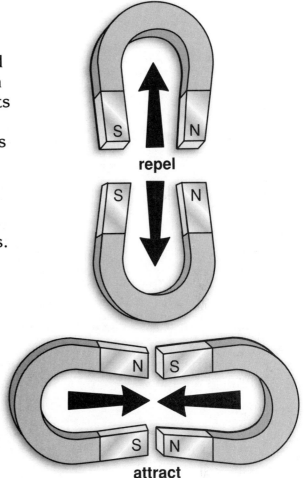

repel

attract

Use the paragraph to answer each question.

1. What are the two ends of a magnet called? _____
   _____
   _____

2. What does it mean when two magnets repel each other? _____
   _____
   _____

3. What does it mean when two magnets attract each other? _____
   _____
   _____

4. How do scientists think some animals use magnets to migrate? _____
   _____
   _____

To correct each sentence, cross out the underlined word.
Then write an antonym above the word.

 1 Each <u>beginning</u> of a magnet is called a pole.

 2 Magnets <u>never</u> have a north and a south pole.

 3 The <u>weakest</u> push or pull on a magnet happens at its poles.

 4 When two magnets repel each other, they move <u>together</u>.

 5 When two magnets attract each other, they move <u>apart</u>.

 6 Two magnets with opposite poles <u>repel</u> each other.

 7 Two magnets with like poles <u>attract</u> each other.

 8 The earth has a north and a <u>north</u> pole.

 9 Some animals have magnets in their bodies that help them migrate in the <u>wrong</u> direction.

 10 The magnets that are in the bodies of some animals are <u>big</u>.

Bonus

Do you think that magnetism is important to everyday life? Make a list of all the good things about magnetism.

It's Shocking!

Electricity was experimented with over 1,000 years before Benjamin Franklin was born.

Several thousand years ago, the ancient Greeks observed electricity. First, they rubbed a hard substance called amber with a cloth. Then they saw that small, lightweight objects were drawn to the amber. What the Greeks witnessed was static electricity. All matter is made up of tiny atoms. Atoms contain even smaller particles, including electrons and protons. Electrons have a negative charge; protons have a positive charge. If an atom loses or gains an electron, it becomes electrically charged. When the ancient Greeks rubbed cloth on the amber, it gained electrons from the cloth. The amber became electrically charged. It could then pick up light objects, such as feathers and straw!

Label each statement as "sometimes," "always," or "never."

_____ 1. Matter is made up of tiny atoms.

_____ 2. Atoms have an electric charge.

_____ 3. Rubbing a cloth on amber makes it able to pick up light objects.

_____ 4. Amber can pick up a heavy piece of metal.

_____ 5. An atom can gain or lose an electron.

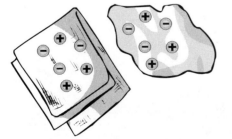  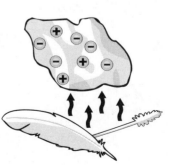

It's Shocking!

Complete the sentences by matching each letter to a numbered line below.

Code

A = 462		N = 115
C = 450		O = 288
E = 357		R = 147
G = 544		S = 170
I = 72		T = 1,816

1. Electricity was first observed by the ancient __ __ __ __ K __.

       544 147 357 357   170

2. __ __ __ __ __ __ electricity is electricity that does not move.

170 1,816 462 1,816 72 450

3. All matter is made up of __ __ __ M __.

    462 1,816 288   170

4. In an U __ __ H __ __ __ __ D atom, there are the same number of protons and

    115 450   462 147 544 357

electrons.

5. Electricity is created when __ L __ __ __ __ __ __ are either lost or gained.

    357   357 450 1,816 147 288 115 170

6. An electron has a negative __ H __ __ __ __.

    450   462 147 544 357

Bonus

Research atoms with a partner. Then, on the back of this page, draw a picture of an atom and label each of its main parts.

The Fascinating Facts About Science Game

Getting Ready to Play

1. Make a copy of the game cards on pages 106–120. Laminate the cards for durability.
2. Divide students into teams of two to four players each.
3. Sort the cards into three stacks: true/false, multiple choice, and fill in the blank.
4. Explain the point system to students:
   true/false = 5 points
   multiple choice = 10 points
   fill in the blank = 15 points

How to Play

1. Player 1 on Team 1 chooses the type of question he wants to answer: true/false, multiple choice, or fill in the blank.
2. The teacher reads aloud the question on the top card of the appropriate stack. If the player answers correctly, his team receives the appropriate number of points.
3. If that player answers incorrectly, Player 1 on Team 2 gets an opportunity to answer the question correctly and earn points for his team. (If the question was a true/false question, the opponent will automatically get it correct if he was listening.) If he answers incorrectly, no team earns the points and the teacher gives the correct answer.
4. The game continues with a player from Team 3 choosing the type of question he wants to answer.
5. The first team to earn 50 points wins. To extend the game, play until one team earns 100 points.

Variation

Use the game cards as flash cards with the whole class. Shuffle all of the cards into one stack and ask one question at a time from the top of the deck. Award one point for each correct answer. Use the game to review just the topic(s) you've recently covered or use all the cards as a fun year-end review.

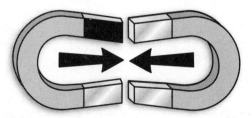

Game Cards

True or False:

The dormouse eats many mushrooms to prepare for hibernation.

(False)

TEC61066

The movement of gray whales from the northern Pacific Ocean to the south is called (migration).

TEC61066

During the winter, the hibernating dormouse lives off _____.

(a) nuts and berries
(b) roots and leaves
(c) stored fat

TEC61066

True or False:

The frilled lizard growls to frighten away its enemies.

(False)

TEC61066

The nocturnal dormouse is active during the (night).

TEC61066

To scare predators, the frilled lizard _____.

(a) expands its neck frill
(b) flies
(c) spits

TEC61066

True or False:

A layer of blubber helps a gray whale survive during the winter.

(True)

TEC61066

The frilled lizard expands its neck frill, hisses, opens its yellow-lined mouth and shows its teeth, and thumps its tail to (frighten) predators.

TEC61066

Gray whales migrate south during the winter to ___.
(a) ride the waves of southern California
(b) give birth in warmer waters
(c) feast on shrimplike krill

TEC61066

True or False:

It is believed that the monarch butterfly tastes bad to predators.

(True)

TEC61066

SURVIVAL & ADAPTATION

Animals use mimicry to
_____.

(a) **fool predators**
(b) entertain other animals
(c) find food

TEC61066

SURVIVAL & ADAPTATION

True or False:

A chameleon has one thick layer of skin.

(False)

TEC61066

SURVIVAL & ADAPTATION

The viceroy butterfly uses (<u>mimicry</u>) to keep predators away.

TEC61066

SURVIVAL & ADAPTATION

Chameleons change color when _____.

(a) they are threatened
(b) there is a change in light or temperature
(c) both a and b

TEC61066

SURVIVAL & ADAPTATION

True or False:

Walking sticks eat during the daytime.

(False)

TEC61066

SURVIVAL & ADAPTATION

A chameleon's basic color helps it blend into its (<u>habitat</u>).

TEC61066

SURVIVAL & ADAPTATION

Walking sticks avoid predators by _____.

(a) running away
(b) looking like a twig
(c) swinging on trees

TEC61066

SURVIVAL & ADAPTATION

True or False:

Compared to other beetles, the Goliath beetle is small.

(False)

TEC61066

SURVIVAL & ADAPTATION

Walking sticks live where the (<u>climate</u>) is tropical or temperate.

TEC61066

SURVIVAL & ADAPTATION

The exoskeleton of the Goliath beetle is _____.

(a) waterproof
(b) soft
(c) both a and b

TEC61066

Game Cards

SURVIVAL & ADAPTATION

The two leathery front wings of the Goliath beetle (protect) its fragile back wings.

TEC61066

SURVIVAL & ADAPTATION

A skunk's spray _____.

(a) is harmless
(b) smells sweet
(c) keeps predators away

TEC61066

SURVIVAL & ADAPTATION

True or False:

Some people think that an opossum is dead because they cannot tell whether it is breathing.

(True)

TEC61066

SURVIVAL & ADAPTATION

The skunk first warns its foes to (stay away) by hissing, growling, and stamping its feet.

TEC61066

SURVIVAL & ADAPTATION

After all danger has passed, an opossum _____.

(a) sometimes attacks its predator
(b) finds food to eat
(c) awakes and escapes

TEC61066

SURVIVAL & ADAPTATION

True or False:

Gibbons live in trees close to the ground so they can spot food on the forest floor.

(False)

TEC61066

SURVIVAL & ADAPTATION

An opossum goes limp, falls to its side, hangs its tongue out, and enters a comalike state to mimic (death).

TEC61066

SURVIVAL & ADAPTATION

Gibbons sing to each other to _____.

(a) put their babies to sleep
(b) bond with each other and mark their territories
(c) exercise their vocal chords

TEC61066

SURVIVAL & ADAPTATION

True or False:

A skunk uses its spray to attract a mate.

(False)

TEC61066

SURVIVAL & ADAPTATION

Gibbons are endangered because (people) hunt them and destroy their habitat.

TEC61066

SURVIVAL & ADAPTATION

True or False:

Impalas leap and run in zigzag patterns to escape predators.

(True)

TEC61066

SURVIVAL & ADAPTATION

The animals that prey upon impalas are _____.

(a) eagles, lions, and pythons
(b) bears, badgers, and foxes
(c) elephants, tigers, and hawks

TEC61066

SURVIVAL & ADAPTATION

An impala can jump ten feet into the air to (escape) a foe.

TEC61066

ECOSYSTEMS

True or False:

The tropical rain forest contains about 6% of all of the earth's species.

(False)

TEC61066

ECOSYSTEMS

About how many new frog species were found in Sri Lanka in 2002?

(a) 50
(b) 6
(c) 100

TEC61066

ECOSYSTEMS

Rain forests have several (layers) of plants, which help feed and protect many kinds of animals.

TEC61066

ECOSYSTEMS

True or False:

Without leaves for photosynthesis, deciduous trees are dormant in winter.

(True)

TEC61066

ECOSYSTEMS

Some deciduous trees draw _____ from their leaves in the fall.

(a) chlorophyll
(b) roots
(c) photosynthesis

TEC61066

ECOSYSTEMS

Deciduous trees lose their leaves in the fall and grow new ones in the (spring).

TEC61066

ECOSYSTEMS

True or False:

Grasslands feed most of the world.

(True)

TEC61066

Game Cards

ECOSYSTEMS — _____ of Earth's land is covered by grasslands.

(a) 10 percent
(b) 25 percent
(c) 50 percent

TEC61066

ECOSYSTEMS — **True or False:**

Large plants can grow in the tundra.

(False)

TEC61066

ECOSYSTEMS — Grasslands have (three or four) layers.

TEC61066

ECOSYSTEMS — Permafrost is _____.

(a) a layer of frost on the surface of a pond in winter
(b) a permanently frozen iceberg in the Arctic
(c) a layer of frozen soil in the tundra

TEC61066

ECOSYSTEMS — **True or False:**

Some animals in the desert estivate, or become inactive, when the weather gets too cold.

(False)

TEC61066

ECOSYSTEMS — Winter brings months of (darkness) to the tundra.

TEC61066

ECOSYSTEMS — A desert normally receives less than _____ of rain a year.

(a) 10 inches
(b) 10 centimeters
(c) 100 inches

TEC61066

ECOSYSTEMS — **True or False:**

In the taiga, the temperature is below freezing for more than half of the year.

(True)

TEC61066

ECOSYSTEMS — Some animals get water from the (plants) they eat in the desert.

TEC61066

ECOSYSTEMS — The _____ is not a coniferous tree.

(a) spruce
(b) sycamore
(c) pine

TEC61066

ECOSYSTEMS — The taiga lies between the deciduous forest and the (tundra). TEC61066	**WEATHER** — The layer of the atmosphere where weather occurs is the _____. (a) stratosphere **(b) troposphere** (c) thermosphere TEC61066
ECOSYSTEMS — **True or False:** Some large coral reefs can be seen from space. **(True)** TEC61066	**WEATHER** — The atmosphere is held in place by (gravity). TEC61066
ECOSYSTEMS — Stony corals live in saltwater that is _____. **(a) warm and shallow** (b) warm and deep (c) cool and shallow TEC61066	**WEATHER** — **True or False:** All clouds form in the same basic way. **(True)** TEC61066
ECOSYSTEMS — Coral reefs are formed from the (skeletons) of coral polyps. TEC61066	**WEATHER** — The type of cloud that forms at ground level is _____. (a) cirrus (b) cumulus **(c) fog** TEC61066
WEATHER — **True or False:** The ozone in the stratosphere helps protect the earth from the sun. **(True)** TEC61066	**WEATHER** — When water vapor turns into liquid and mixes with dust, (clouds) form. TEC61066

Game Cards

True or False:

Snow is freezing rain that falls to the earth.

(False)

TEC61066

Winds blow from high pressure to (low pressure).

TEC61066

If the temperature in the clouds is above freezing, the precipitation will be _____.

(a) snow
(b) sleet
(c) rain

TEC61066

True or False:

Scientists study clues from the past to learn more about the climates of the present and the future.

(True)

TEC61066

The only liquid form of precipitation is (rain).

TEC61066

Scientists get clues about the climates of the past from _____.

(a) keys
(b) ships' logs
(c) town maps

TEC61066

True or False:

Prevailing winds change often.

(False)

TEC61066

Climate is the average of all (weather) over a length of time.

TEC61066

The winds that are most helpful to sailing ships are the _____.

(a) horse latitudes
(b) trade winds
(c) prevailing westerlies

TEC61066

True or False:

The biggest threats from a hurricane are high winds, heavy rain, flooding, storm surges, and tornadoes.

(True)

TEC61066

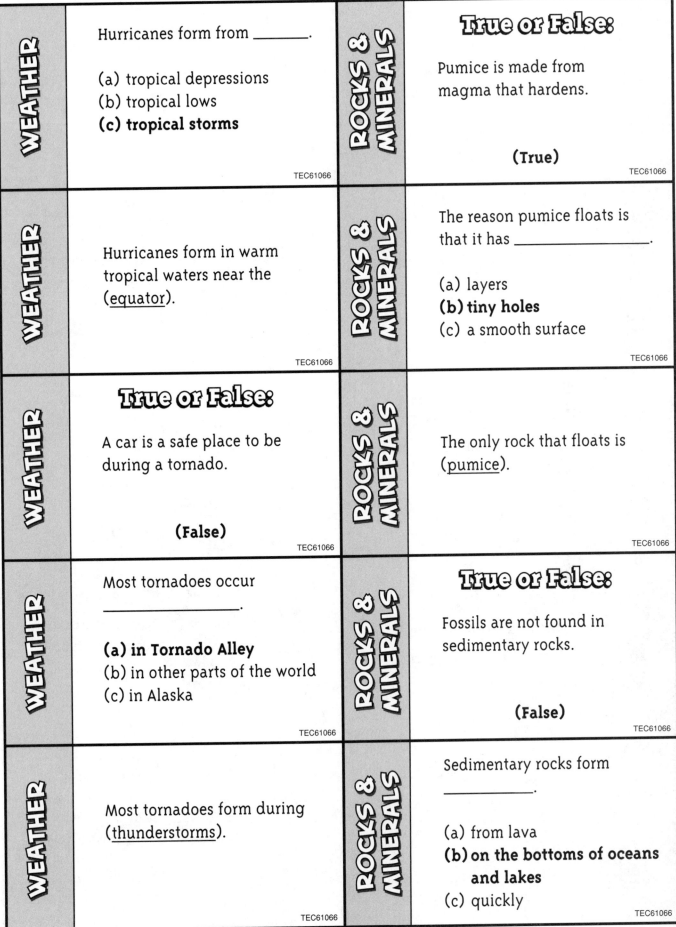

WEATHER

Hurricanes form from _____.

(a) tropical depressions
(b) tropical lows
(c) tropical storms

TEC61066

WEATHER

Hurricanes form in warm tropical waters near the (equator).

TEC61066

WEATHER

True or False:

A car is a safe place to be during a tornado.

(False)

TEC61066

WEATHER

Most tornadoes occur _____.

(a) in Tornado Alley
(b) in other parts of the world
(c) in Alaska

TEC61066

WEATHER

Most tornadoes form during (thunderstorms).

TEC61066

ROCKS & MINERALS

True or False:

Pumice is made from magma that hardens.

(True)

TEC61066

ROCKS & MINERALS

The reason pumice floats is that it has _____.

(a) layers
(b) tiny holes
(c) a smooth surface

TEC61066

ROCKS & MINERALS

The only rock that floats is (pumice).

TEC61066

ROCKS & MINERALS

True or False:

Fossils are not found in sedimentary rocks.

(False)

TEC61066

ROCKS & MINERALS

Sedimentary rocks form _____.

(a) from lava
(b) on the bottoms of oceans and lakes
(c) quickly

TEC61066

Game Cards

ROCKS & MINERALS	It takes (<u>thousands</u>) of years for sedimentary rocks to form. TEC61066
ROCKS & MINERALS	The atoms of minerals are arranged in _____. (a) fossils (b) gems **(c) crystals** TEC61066
ROCKS & MINERALS	### True or False: A metamorphic rock is one that has been changed from one kind of rock into another. **(True)** TEC61066
ROCKS & MINERALS	The only mineral that is hard enough to cut a diamond is (<u>another diamond</u>). TEC61066
ROCKS & MINERALS	To change an igneous or sedimentary rock into a metamorphic rock, _____. (a) marble is needed (b) slate is needed **(c) heat and/or pressure is needed** TEC61066
EARTH'S SURFACE	### True or False: The layer under the crust is called the mantle. **(True)** TEC61066
ROCKS & MINERALS	Every (<u>metamorphic</u>) rock used to be an igneous, a sedimentary, or another metamorphic rock. TEC61066
EARTH'S SURFACE	The earth's crust is divided into _____. (a) mantles **(b) plates** (c) rocks TEC61066
ROCKS & MINERALS	### True or False: A soft mineral like talc can be scratched with a fingernail. **(True)** TEC61066
EARTH'S SURFACE	The thin layer of the earth we walk on is called the (<u>crust</u>). TEC61066

EARTH'S SURFACE

True or False:

Most earthquakes are big.

(False)

TEC61066

EARTH'S SURFACE

The hot melted rock that flows out of a volcano is called (lava).

TEC61066

EARTH'S SURFACE

A break in the earth's crust is called _____.

(a) an earthquake
(b) a fault
(c) a pressure point

TEC61066

EARTH'S SURFACE

True or False:

All mountains are formed in the same way.

(False)

TEC61066

EARTH'S SURFACE

When the earth's plates move, (pressure) builds on the rocks along the faults.

TEC61066

EARTH'S SURFACE

Mountains wear away because of _____.

(a) rocky layers pushing against each other
(b) erosion
(c) folding

TEC61066

EARTH'S SURFACE

True or False:

Volcanoes can never become extinct.

(False)

TEC61066

EARTH'S SURFACE

Low, round mountains have been worn down by (erosion).

TEC61066

EARTH'S SURFACE

The bowl shape that forms at the top of a volcano after it erupts is called a _____.

(a) crater
(b) ladle
(c) mug

TEC61066

SOLAR SYSTEM

True or False:

Earth is the center of our solar system.

(False)

TEC61066

Game Cards

SOLAR SYSTEM

Some experts do not think that
_____ is a real planet.

(a) Jupiter
(b) Neptune
(c) Pluto

TEC61066

SOLAR SYSTEM

True or False:

The moon is bright because
it reflects light from nearby
stars.

(False)

TEC61066

SOLAR SYSTEM

Many planetlike objects lie
beyond (Neptune).

TEC61066

SOLAR SYSTEM

The shape changes that the
moon goes through are called
_____.

(a) eclipses
(b) phases
(c) orbits

TEC61066

SOLAR SYSTEM

True or False:

Earth is the best planet in
our solar system for living
things.

(True)

TEC61066

SOLAR SYSTEM

The brightest object in our
night sky is the (moon).

TEC61066

SOLAR SYSTEM

The atmosphere _____.

(a) filters the sun's strong rays
(b) protects us from the moon's
beams
(c) does not provide Earth with
clean air

TEC61066

SOLAR SYSTEM

True or False:

All stars are the same size,
color, and brightness.

(False)

TEC61066

SOLAR SYSTEM

The only planet in our solar
system that can support life is
(Earth).

TEC61066

SOLAR SYSTEM

Stars with the coolest
temperatures are _____.

(a) yellow
(b) red
(c) blue

TEC61066

SOLAR SYSTEM

Stars are large balls of hot (gases) in the sky.

TEC61066

SOLAR SYSTEM

Most asteroids can be found _____.

(a) in Jupiter's orbit
(b) in the Main Belt
(c) close to the sun

TEC61066

SOLAR SYSTEM

True or False:

Comets are made of ice and dust.

(True)

TEC61066

SOLAR SYSTEM

Asteroids can be a few feet in size or up to (hundreds) of miles long.

TEC61066

SOLAR SYSTEM

Comets can be seen when they are near _____.

(a) the sun
(b) a planet
(c) a moon

TEC61066

SOLAR SYSTEM

True or False:

A meteorite is a meteor that crashes into another meteor.

(False)

TEC61066

SOLAR SYSTEM

The famous comet that comes past Earth about every 76 years is (Halley's comet).

TEC61066

SOLAR SYSTEM

A meteor is sometimes called _____.

(a) lightning
(b) a comet
(c) a shooting star

TEC61066

SOLAR SYSTEM

True or False:

Asteroids are minor planets that orbit the sun.

(True)

TEC61066

SOLAR SYSTEM

As soon as most meteors enter Earth's atmosphere, they get very hot and (burn up).

TEC61066

Game Cards

	True or False:		The (molecules) in a liquid are farther apart than in a solid.
MATTER	A solid's molecules are far apart. **(False)** TEC61066	**MATTER**	 TEC61066

	_____ is an example of a solid. **(a) A rock** (b) Air (c) Water TEC61066		**True or False:**
MATTER		**MATTER**	Gas particles move quickly. **(True)** TEC61066

			A gas is a kind of _____. (a) molecule **(b) matter** (c) air
MATTER	A solid has a definite volume and (shape). TEC61066	**MATTER**	 TEC61066

	True or False:		
MATTER	Liquids are usually as strong as solids. **(False)** TEC61066	**MATTER**	Gas particles move more (slowly) if the gas is cold. TEC61066

	The liquid form of ice is _____ _____. (a) vapor **(b) water** (c) snow TEC61066		**True or False:**
MATTER		**MATTER**	A mixture can be separated into separate substances. **(True)** TEC61066

MATTER

Water is made of _____ kind(s) of molecule.

(a) two
(b) one
(c) three

TEC61066

ENERGY & MOTION

True or False:

Heat always travels from colder to hotter substances.

(False)

TEC61066

MATTER

The air that we breathe is a mixture of (gases).

TEC61066

ENERGY & MOTION

When fast-moving molecules collide with slow-moving molecules, the slower molecules _____.

(a) stay the same temperature
(b) get colder
(c) get warmer

TEC61066

MATTER

True or False:

The solute is easy to separate from the solvent in a solution.

(False)

TEC61066

ENERGY & MOTION

The hotter a substance is, the (faster) its molecules move.

TEC61066

MATTER

The part of the solution that dissolves is called a _____.

(a) solute
(b) solvent
(c) molecule

TEC61066

ENERGY & MOTION

True or False:

We can live without light.

(False)

TEC61066

MATTER

Every solution has (two) main parts.

TEC61066

ENERGY & MOTION

Two types of light sources are _____.

(a) natural and man-made
(b) plants and natural
(c) man-made and animals

TEC61066

Game Cards

ENERGY & MOTION

Light is a form of (<u>radiant</u>) energy.

TEC61066

ENERGY & MOTION

All magnets have ___ poles.

(a) two
(b) three
(c) four

TEC61066

ENERGY & MOTION

True or False:

Sound travels in waves.

(True)

TEC61066

ENERGY & MOTION

Some (<u>animals</u>) have magnets in their bodies.

TEC61066

ENERGY & MOTION

Sound is caused by a _____ object.

(a) loud
(b) vibrating
(c) still

TEC61066

ENERGY & MOTION

True or False:

An atom never gains or loses electrons.

(False)

TEC61066

ENERGY & MOTION

The ears turn sound waves into signals for the (<u>brain</u>).

TEC61066

ENERGY & MOTION

_____ first observed electricity.

(a) Benjamin Franklin
(b) Americans
(c) Ancient Greeks

TEC61066

ENERGY & MOTION

True or False:

On a magnet, the north pole is attracted to the south pole.

(True)

TEC61066

ENERGY & MOTION

Rubbing amber with a (<u>cloth</u>) makes the amber able to pick up light feathers and straw.

TEC61066

Answer Keys

Page 5

1. The nocturnal dormouse searches for food during the ~~day~~.
   night
2. The dormouse eats ~~less~~ food before hibernating.
   more
3. During hibernation, the dormouse's breathing gets ~~faster~~.
   slower
4. The dormouse's body temperature ~~rises~~ during hibernation.
   drops
5. The hibernating dormouse survives on stored ~~water~~.
   fat
6. The dormouse could starve if it wakes too ~~late~~.
   soon

Page 6

1. WOODCHUCK
2. TOAD
3. DORMOUSE
4. NIGHTHAWK
5. LIZARD
6. GREATER HORSESHOE BAT

Page 7

1. It eats over a ton.
2. They travel more than 5,000 miles.
3. They need blubber to live on during their long journey southward.
4. Answers will vary.

Page 8

1. C
2. D
3. E
4. B
5. A

Page 9

1. large
2. frill, mouth
3. thump
4. bigger
5. runs

Page 10

1. true
2. false
3. false
4. true
5. false
6. false
7. false
8. true

Page 11

1. a
2. b
3. b
4. a

Page 12

1. KING SNAKE
2. LEAF INSECT
3. NEMORIA ARIZONARIA CATERPILLAR
4. MONARCH BUTTERFLY
5. DRONGO BIRD
6. FLY ORCHID
7. ANGLERFISH
8. HOVERFLY

THEY HISS!

Page 13

1. tropical
2. night
3. predators
4. breeze
5. twig

Page 14

1. vine snake
2. crab spider
3. spines
4. crocodile
5. ray
6. bite

g	n	l	e	t	i	b	s	s	c	t	w	a	e
e	l	o	c	o	r	s	o	e	r	n	l	b	c
q	z	l	s	d	p	n	k	l	a	b	l	g	f
k	m	b	p	c	f	a	t	a	b	a	r	y	z
f	i	g	y	o	n	u	z	k	s	r	f	a	s
c	n	n	p	s	l	w	h	e	p	s	j	b	y
p	e	w	e	d	o	q	j	x	i	m	c	n	h
z	o	n	e	c	r	o	c	o	d	i	l	e	k
b	i	r	j	t	l	a	s	e	k	v	y	d
v	m	s	p	i	n	e	s	h	r	o	s	g	t

Page 15

A chameleon has a basic color that helps it blend into its surroundings.
A chameleon has several layers of skin.
A chameleon changes colors when threatened.
A chameleon changes color when the air gets colder.
A chameleon changes color when the light changes.

Page 16

1. chameleon
2. polecat
3. black moth
4. ptarmigan
5. praying mantis
6. tiger
7. sloth
8. flatfish

Page 17
1. The Goliath beetle has a ~~soft~~ exoskeleton.
                   hard
2. The beetle's front wings help ~~move~~ its hind wings.
                     protect
3. The Goliath beetle ~~exercises~~ in order to grow.
                   molts
4. The beetle's ~~mother~~ covers and protects it.
                   exoskeleton
5. Adult Goliath beetles eat fruit and ~~flowers~~.
                   tree sap

Page 18
1. clam
2. turtle
3. armadillo
4. hedgehog

Page 19
1. fact (blue)
2. opinion (red)
3. opinion (red)
4. fact (blue)
5. fact (blue)
6. opinion (red)
7. fact (blue)
8. opinion (red)

Page 20
Statements 2, 3, and 5 should be crossed out.

Page 21
1. c
2. b
3. a
4. b

Page 22
1. ZORILLA
2. SPITTING COBRA
3. SQUID
4. POISON DART FROG
5. FIRE SALAMANDER

Page 23
1. Gibbons live in the rain forest canopy high above the ground.
2. Singing helps gibbons bond and mark their territory.
3. Humans hunt gibbons and cut down the rain forests where the gibbons live.
4. leopards and pythons
5. Gibbons swing with their arms from one tree branch to another.

Page 24
1. FAMILY
2. RAIN FOREST
3. CANOPY
4. BUDS
5. EDGES
6. HIDE
7. TREETOPS
8. ABOVE
9. BRACHIATORS
10. AVOID

Page 25
1. sometimes
2. always
3. sometimes
4. never
5. sometimes

Page 26
1. F
2. D
3. E
4. A
5. C
6. B

Page 27
1. It is a rain forest.
2. Answers will vary.
3. It has many different species and gets a lot of rain and sun.
4. Answers will vary.

Page 28
1. howler monkey
2. toucan
3. tamandua
4. tree boa constrictor
5. jaguar
6. leaf-cutter ant

Page 29
1. b
2. a
3. c
4. a

Page 30
1. In fall, the days grow <u>shorter</u>.
2. Some deciduous trees take back <u>chlorophyll</u> from their leaves.
3. The colorful leaves soon die and <u>fall</u> from the tree.
4. During the winter when the tree is bare, <u>photosynthesis</u> ends.
5. Winter ends, and the days get <u>warmer</u>.
6. New <u>buds</u> form on the trees.
7. The buds turn into <u>green</u> leaves.
8. The green leaves absorb energy and grow through the <u>summer</u>.

Page 31
1. false
2. true
3. true
4. false
5. true

Page 32
1. seeds
2. blades
3. stem
4. stolen
5. shoots
6. rhizome
7. roots

Page 33
1. adaptations
2. arid
3. sandstorm
4. estivate
5. oasis

Page 34
1. Drink
2. Burrow
3. Cactus
4. Feet
5. Humps
6. Warm
7. Feathers

Page 35
Answers will vary.

	Spring/Summer	Fall/Winter
Sunlight	The tundra has more hours of daylight. The sun shines all the time in summer.	The hours of daylight decrease. The tundra is mostly dark for several months.
Temperature	It is warm enough for plants to grow. The permafrost does not melt.	It is too cold for most animals to remain and plants to grow. The permafrost does not melt.
Plants	Dormant plants become active again. New plants grow. Large plants still cannot grow because the roots cannot go through the permafrost.	Many plants are dormant.
Animals	Some animals' fur changes from white to brown. Animals migrate to the tundra.	Some animals' fur turns white to blend in with the snow. Many animals migrate away from the tundra.

Page 36

Ⓢ N O W   G O O S E
C Ⓤ R L E W
T R U Ⓜ P E T E R   S W A N
Ⓜ O O S E
R Ⓔ D   F O X
C Ⓡ A N E

S N O W Ⓨ   O W L
H A R Ⓔ
W E Ⓐ S E L
P O L A Ⓡ   B E A R
Ⓒ
P T A Ⓡ M I G A N
W Ⓞ L F
M Ⓤ S K   O X
R A V E Ⓝ
R E Ⓓ P O L L

Page 37
Answers will vary. Possible answers include the following:
1. Cone-bearing trees grow in the taiga. They have green needlelike leaves all year long.
2. A conifer has cones, needlelike leaves, and downward-sloping branches. Most conifers do not lose their leaves in the fall. The leaves of a conifer tree have a waxy coating. A conifer has male and female pinecones.
3. The female cone is large and bears seeds. The male cone is smaller and has pollen. The male cone dies after it scatters the pollen.
4. The taiga is below freezing for more than half of the year.

Page 38

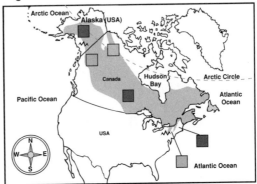

Page 39
1. Coral polyps live in ~~cold~~ warm, shallow saltwater.
2. Coral reefs are made of the skeletons of ~~soft~~ stony coral.
3. The bodies of ~~large~~ small or tiny stony corals build a reef over time.
4. Coral reefs grow ~~quickly~~ slowly.
5. When coral polyps die, they leave behind ~~soft~~ hard skeletons.
6. Coral polyps have ~~cone-shaped~~ tube-shaped bodies.

Page 40
1. starfish
2. octopus
3. lined seahorse
4. hermit crab
5. shark
6. brain coral
7. damselfish
8. shrimp
9. sea anemone
<u>Australia</u>

Page 41

Answers may vary. Possible answers include the following:
1. Because the earth has gravity, the earth's atmosphere <u>is held in place</u>.
2. Since scientists study changes that occur in the first layer, <u>weather forecasts can be made</u>.
3. If a meteor enters the third layer of the earth's atmosphere, it will most likely be <u>burned up</u>.
4. We can stay in touch with people all over the world because the fourth layer of air <u>bounces radio waves back to the earth</u>.
5. If we did not have the second layer of air, <u>we would suffer greater damage from the sun's harmful rays</u>.

Page 42
1. hygrometer, humidity
2. barometer, air pressure
3. rain gauge, precipitation
4. thermometer, temperature
5. wind vane, wind direction
6. anemometer, wind speed

Page 43

Answers may vary.
1. Water vapor is a gas that forms when water from oceans, lakes, rivers, and ponds evaporates.
2. warm air
3. It changes into a liquid and mixes with the dust in the air.
4. Fog forms near the ground; other types of clouds form higher in the air.
5. The weather and the height at which water vapor condenses determine which types of clouds form.

Page 44
1. a
2. b
3. b
4. b
5. a

The scientist's name is <u>Luke Howard</u>.

Page 45
1. water
2. warm
3. freeze
4. cold
5. larger

Page 46
1. snowflakes
2. sleet
3. hailstones
4. evaporate
5. precipitation
6. vapor
7. clouds
8. condenses
9. rain

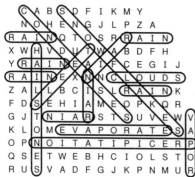

Page 47
1. F
2. F
3. F
4. T
5. F

Page 48
1. Sea Breeze
2. warm air rising
3. cool air sinking
4. cool air sinking
5. warm air rising
6. Land Breeze

Page 49
1. b, a ship's diary
2. a, two centuries
3. b, average
4. c, fossils and written records

Page 50
1. mammoth—frozen specimens with wooly coats
2. weather balloon—floats in the atmosphere to gather clues about weather
3. tree ring—shows one year of growth; wide = warm and wet, good growth; narrow = cold and dry, poor growth
4. ocean buoy—floats in water to record temperatures and measure other conditions of the atmosphere
5. amber—hardened sap, survives millions of years, often has insects and air bubbles inside
6. satellite—orbits in space and sends data about weather and temperatures on Earth
7. glacier—shows what the climate was like when the water froze

Page 51
1. equator
2. hurricane
3. tropical storm
4. tropical depression

Page 52
1. surge
2. damage
3. inches
4. flooding
5. around
6. strength
7. destroy
8. winds
9. trees
10. before

<u>thunderstorms</u>

Page 53
1. sometimes
2. never
3. always
4. sometimes
5. always

Page 54
1. W
2. A
3. S
4. H
5. I
6. N
7. G
8. T
9. O
10. N

OKLAHOMA CITY

Page 55
1. F
2. F
3. T
4. F
5. F
6. F

Page 56
1. fact (brown)
2. fact (brown)
3. fact (brown)
4. opinion (gray)
5. opinion (gray)
6. opinion (gray)
7. fact (brown)
8. opinion (gray)
9. fact (brown)
10. opinion (gray)

Page 57
                thousands
1. Sedimentary rocks take ~~hundreds~~ of years to form.

2. Fossils form over time when dead plants and animals get
                      sediment
covered by layers of ~~lava~~.
          top
3. The weight of the ~~lower~~ layers of sediment presses the bottom

layers together.
               bottom
4. Sedimentary rocks can form at the ~~top~~ of river valleys.
     type
5. The ~~size~~ of sedimentary rock that is formed depends on the

minerals that are pressed together.

Page 58
Sedimentary: 1, 3, 4, 6, 8, 9
Not sedimentary: 2, 5, 7

Page 59
1. a
2. b
3. b
4. a
5. b

Page 60
1. marble
2. phyllite
3. recycled
4. heat, pressure
5. slate
6. igneous, sedimentary
7. gneiss
8. limestone

Michelangelo

Page 61
1. quartz
2. crystals
3. minerals
4. diamonds
5. talc
6. limestone

Page 62

Mohs' Hardness Scale	
Hardness	Mineral
1	talc
2	gypsum
3	calcite
4	fluorite
5	apatite
6	orthoclase
7	quartz
8	topaz
9	corundum
10	diamond

1. corundum, diamond
2. calcite, gypsum, talc
3. diamond
4. talc
5. calcite

Page 63
          top
1. The ~~bottom~~ layer of the earth is called the crust.
               curved
2. The crust is divided into ~~flat~~ plates.
               hot
3. There is a layer of ~~cold~~ syrupy rock under the crust.
                    mantle
4. The layer under the crust is called the ~~plate~~.
               thin
5. The earth's crust is ~~thick~~ and hard.
              bottom
6. The rocks on the ~~top~~ of the crust are hot.

Page 64
Across
2—crust
3—slides
7—continents
8—plate

Down
1—floor
4—slowly
5—three
6—mantle

The crust under the oceans is <u>thinner</u> than the crust under the continents.

Page 65
1. movement
2. pressure
3. vibrations
4. crust
5. plates

Page 66
1. fact
2. fact
3. opinion
4. fact
5. fact
6. opinion
7. fact
8. fact

seismographs

Page 67
1. Hot gases build up inside the earth.
2. A rocky tube forms, leading to the surface.
3. Magma and hot gases erupt through a vent.
4. Lava burns trees and buildings.
5. A crater forms.

Page 68
1. composite volcano
2. shield volcano
3. cinder cone volcano

Page 69
1. a
2. b
3. c
4. b
5. a
6. c

Page 70
Water
- rain
- rivers and streams running over the earth's surface
- groundwater that causes limestone to dissolve
- ocean waves that crash against rocks and shorelines

Wind
- dunes being moved from place to place
- air that blows and carries away loose bits of rock and soil
- air taking away sand from a desert floor

Ice
- valley glaciers
- continental glaciers

Page 71
1. true
2. false
3. false
4. false
5. true

Page 72
1. Mars
2. Mercury
3. Neptune
4. Jupiter
5. Earth
6. Saturn
7. Uranus
8. Venus

COPERNICUS

Page 73
1. b
2. c
3. a
4. b

Page 74
1. shuttle
2. lights
3. winds
4. Meteor
5. ozone
6. Airplanes
7. weather
8. greenhouse

Page 75
1. The moon has phases because the amount of sunlight the moon reflects toward Earth changes as the moon orbits Earth.
2. It takes the moon about a month to make one trip around Earth.
3. The moon is in Earth's shadow during a lunar eclipse.
4. Earth keeps sunlight from shining on the moon during a lunar eclipse.
5. The moon reflects light from the sun.

Page 76
In a lunar eclipse, Earth blocks sunlight from the moon. The moon is in complete darkness and has a red glow.

In a solar eclipse, the moon blocks sunlight from Earth. The moon casts a shadow on Earth.

Page 77
1. About 3,000 stars can be seen without a telescope on a clear night.
2. Stars are large balls of hot gases.
3. Stars shine because intense heat causes them to glow.
4. Red stars are cooler than the sun.
5. Some stars are bigger than the sun.

Page 78

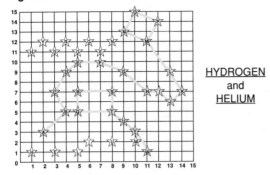

HYDROGEN
and
HELIUM

Page 79
1. No. A comet can only be seen without a telescope when it is near the sun.
2. Yes. Halley's comet returns about every 76 years.
3. Yes. Over time, a comet could lose all of its ice. It could also crash into a planet or moon and be destroyed.
4. Yes. Some comets can be ten miles wide.

Page 80
1. Comets cannot be seen without a telescope until they get close to the sun.
2. When a comet is far away from the sun, it does not have a tail.
3. A comet's orbit usually has an oval shape.
4. As a comet nears the sun, a tail begins to form.
5. Some comets have two tails: one of gas and another of dust.
6. Comets can collide with planets or moons and leave craters.
7. A comet's tail can sometimes be 100 million miles long.
8. Comets begin to lose their tails as they start to move away from the sun.
9. A comet travels back to the outer edge of our solar system.

Page 81
1. b
2. a
3. b
4. c

Page 82
1801—The first asteroid, Ceres, was identified 195 years before the NEAR spacecraft was launched.
1891—Ninety years after the first asteroid was spotted, a man named Max Wolf found asteroids by using a telescope to take pictures of the sky.
1908—One hundred seven years after the first asteroid was identified, nearly 50 square miles of land was burned when an asteroid exploded above Russia.
1993—In 1993, scientists saw for the first time a moon orbiting an asteroid.
1996—The Near-Earth Asteroid Rendezvous (NEAR) spacecraft was launched in 1996.
2001—A U.S. spacecraft landed on an asteroid for the first time four years before a Japanese spacecraft did.
2005—A Japanese probe landed on an asteroid and sent back detailed pictures.

Page 83
1. Meteors look like a ~~slow~~ quick streak of light in the sky.
2. A meteor turns into a ~~comet~~ meteorite once it reaches Earth.
3. Meteors can weigh as ~~little~~ much as 300,000 tons.
4. Meteors are usually made from pieces of asteroids, comets, or pieces of the same material from which ~~meteors~~ planets are made.
5. Most meteors ~~freeze~~ burn before we can see them.

Page 84
1. SHOOTING STARS
2. METEOR SHOWER
3. ANTARCTICA
4. PIECES OF ASTEROIDS OR COMETS
5. OVER ONE HUNDRED TWENTY

A	B	C	D	E	F	G	H	I	J	K	L	M	N	O	P	Q	R	S	T	U	V	W	X	Y	Z
3	6	9	12	15	18	21	24	27	30	33	36	39	42	45	48	51	54	57	60	63	66	69	72	75	78

Page 85
1. A solid's molecules are packed closely together and move slowly back and forth. A solid is strong and has a definite shape and volume.
2. Solids do not look or feel the same. Some solids stretch, some break, and some are clear.
3. Force is needed to change a solid's shape.
4. Answers will vary.

Page 86
1. vibrate
2. solid
3. volume
4. physical
5. ice
6. resist
7. shape
8. atoms

Its shape!

Page 87
1. Liquids take the ~~size~~ shape of the container they are in.
2. A liquid is usually ~~stronger~~ weaker than a solid.
3. When water changes into a solid, it is called ~~steam~~ ice.
4. Molecules are not packed closely together in a ~~solid~~ liquid.

Page 88
1. PARTICLES, SOLID, GAS
2. SHAPE, DEFINITE SHAPE
3. STRONGER, SQUEEZED
4. WATER, LIQUID
5. GASES, SOLIDS

Page 89

	Solid	Liquid	Gas
Shape	definite shape	no definite shape—takes shape of its container	no definite size or shape
Movement of Particles	particles vibrate back and forth but stay in the same place	particles move back and forth and from place to place	particles move all the time, colliding and bouncing about
Space	always takes up the same amount of space	always takes up the same amount of space	particles fully fill a container, no matter the size

Page 90
1. false
2. true
3. false
4. false
5. true
6. true
7. true
8. false

127

Page 91
1. mixture
2. liquid
3. solid
4. gases
5. physical

Page 92
1. fact (blue)
2. opinion (red)
3. opinion (red)
4. fact (blue)
5. fact (blue)
6. opinion (red)
7. fact (blue)
8. fact (blue)

Page 93
1. e
2. d
3. a
4. b
5. c

Page 94
1. mixtures
2. soluble
3. evenly
4. solvent
5. saturated
6. solute
7. solutions

h	r	e	t	u	l	o	s	v	s
p	e	y	e	b	o	w	f	o	a
s	e	v	n	l	y	k	l	t	t
o	l	r	e	m	k	u	q	a	u
l	b	x	c	n	t	f	a	l	r
v	u	c	o	i	x	b	p	v	a
e	l	a	o	t	z	y	l	u	t
n	o	n	d	s	e	u	e	c	e
t	s	n	b	l	h	f	e	u	d
g	d	m	i	x	t	u	r	e	s

Page 95
Answers may vary.
                                        colder
1. Heat travels from hot objects to ~~hotter~~ objects.
                                        faster
2. The hotter a substance is, the ~~slower~~ its molecules move.
                                                        warmer
3. The ice in a glass of soda melts because the soda is ~~colder~~.
    Heat
4. ~~Ice~~ always travels in one direction.
    Fast
5. ~~Slow~~ moving molecules cause ice to melt.

Page 96

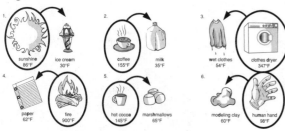

Heat always moves from <u>warmer</u> to <u>colder</u> objects.

Page 97
1. a
2. b
3. c
4. c

Page 98
Earth with light:
    right temperature for life
    day and night
    fall, winter, spring, summer
    working water cycle
    wind and rain
    plenty of food and oxygen

Earth without light:
    too cold for life
    complete darkness
    no seasons
    no water cycle
    no wind or rain
    no food or oxygen

Page 99
1. waves
2. vibrate
3. substance
4. signals
5. sound

Page 100
1. The school bell rings at 3:15 PM.
2. The bell's vibrations cause the air around it to vibrate.
3. The vibrations keep moving through the air as sound waves.
4. The sound waves travel in all directions.
5. The sound waves reach students' ears.
6. The ears turn the vibrations into signals for the students' brains.
7. Their brains decide what sound the students hear.
8. The students leave for home.

Page 101
Answers may vary.
1. They are called north and south poles.
2. When two magnets repel each other, their like poles are lined up and they push away from each other.
3. When two magnets attract each other, their opposite poles are lined up and they pull toward each other.
4. Some animals use magnets to find their way when they migrate.

Page 102
Answers may vary.
1. end
2. always
3. strongest
4. apart
5. together
6. attract
7. repel
8. south
9. right
10. tiny

Page 103
1. always
2. sometimes
3. always
4. never
5. sometimes

Page 104
1. GREEKS
2. STATIC
3. ATOMS
4. UNCHARGED
5. ELECTRONS
6. CHARGE